DELUS

HATJE
CANTZ

Issue 1
Autumn 2024

DELUS

Journal for
Landscape and
Urban Studies

DELUS is an annual publication (digital and print) founded in 2022 by the Institute for Landscape and Urban Studies (LUS) at ETH Zürich that explores emerging themes, topics and methods from landscape and urban studies. It brings academic knowledge to a broader audience and fosters exchange among designers, artists, scientists, scholars and students.

A Note from the Editors

Sara Frikech
Johanna Just

On December 7, 1972, a photograph from the depths of outer space captured our planet. As the crew of Apollo 17 journeyed towards the moon, nearly 29 400 kilometres away, they beheld Earth in its entirety. It appeared small, fragile, yet familiar – like a blue marble nestled in the palm of the universe. This singular image inspired a generation, fostering a sense of global climate awareness. Simultaneously, it drew attention to Earth's unique watery surface. The vivid hues of blue and white unmistakably signify the omnipresence of this vital matter. However, despite the biosphere being hailed as a vital, "self-regulating entity"[1] in line with Gaia theory, which emerged shortly after the image was taken, there remains the potential for water vapour to escape into space if it dissipates rapidly enough into the upper atmosphere. Scientists Lynn Margulis and Stephan Harding, both advocates of Gaia theory, explain this continuous chase for water starting from the origins of planetary life, claiming that "[l]ife ensures its own continuity by retaining and interacting with liquid water on our planet's surface."[2]

As we descend from the cosmic perspective of Apollo 17's iconic 'Blue Marble' image, we zoom in on the deep hues of blue and white of our planet's oceans, embodying the principles of the "oceanic turn"[3] embraced by scholars across disciplines. This paradigm shift represents a departure from traditional land-centric perspectives and emphasizes the significance of oceans in shaping our societies, cultures, histories and environments. Within this vast maritime expanse, topics such as trade and commerce, colonialism and imperialism, environmental degradation and conservation take centre stage, playing a crucial role in today's global interconnectedness. However, the oceanic turn does not solely focus on oceans but encompasses all bodies of water; it is a water-centric approach, seeking insights into the complex relationships between life and wet environments.[4]

1 James Lovelock, *Gaia: A New Look at Life on Earth* (Oxford; New York, NY: Oxford University Press, 1979), ix.

2 Stephan Harding and Lynn Margulis, "Water Gaia: 3.5 Thousand Million Years of Wetness on Planet Earth," in *Gaia in Turmoil: Climate Change, Biodepletion, and Earth Ethics in an Age of Crisis,* ed. Eileen Crist and H. Bruce Rinke (Boston: MIT Press, 2010).

3 To learn more about the "oceanic turn," see: Laura Winkiel, "Introduction," in *English Language Notes* 57, no. 1 (2019): 1–10.

4 To learn more about the notion of wetness, see: Dilip da Cunha (2019), *The Invention of Rivers: Alexander's Eye and Ganga's Descent* (Philadelphia: University of Pennsylvania Press, 2019), 1.

RIGHT
Earth, like a blue marble nestled in the palm of the universe. NASA, AS17-148-22727, 1972.

This includes issues such as water management, water knowledge and practices, environmental justice and the effects of climate change. In other words, understanding our environment necessitates exploring water's myriad forms – liquid and solid, ephemeral and transparent; furthermore, understanding the way we may pursue or repel water involves grasping the living beings within it.

In this first issue of DELUS, we present a collection of writings forming an anthology; these pieces adopt a water-centric lens addressing the notion of 'chasing water.' Nine authors guide us through various bodies of water, allowing us to immerse ourselves in their diverse manifestations. By employing the notion of 'chasing,' we seek to highlight water's role in shaping and sustaining landscape and urban environments, as well as our continuous efforts to influence its course.

Associated with 'pursuit,' the act of chasing water highlights endeavours to seek out, harness and manage water as a resource, securing it for survival, agriculture and industry. This ultimately indicates that "the practices of everyday life ... are predicated upon and conditioned by the supply, circulation, and elimination of water."[5] Water's inherent nature of being hard to contain, instead, conveys a paradox emerging from this metaphorical chase:

> Water deeply at rest is yet always in motion;
> the stillest lake is constantly, invisibly transformed
> into vapour, rising in the air. A river can be dammed
> and diverted, yet its water is incompressible:
> it will not go where there is not room for it.[6]

At times slipping through our fingers and at other times presenting itself as a force to be reckoned with, water has a volatile and unpredictable nature. The contradictory idea of 'chasing water' reflects the challenge of capturing, storing and distributing water in a world where it can be abundant yet inaccessible.

Human efforts to navigate water's destructive potential are encapsulated in the idea of 'chasing it away': this encompasses flood management, drainage systems and other forms of environmental manipulation aimed at protecting human settlements and interests from water's overpowering forces. Finally, the notion of 'chasing water' invites dialogue on the role of water, emphasizing the complexity of our relationship with the element in shaping landscapes, cities and societies. By exploring these varied meanings, the contributions offer insightful perspectives on how we interact with, depend on and envision the future of living with and without water.

The opening essay by Mathilde Redouté delves into the transformation of England's Fens from waterlogged to arable land (p. 14). Following this essay, Akshar Gajjar and Bhavya Jain examine Srinagar's waterways through the craft of a pashmina shawl, challenging hegemonic cartography (p. 24). Valentina Noce embarks on a visual journey, drawing from Pascal's abyss to probe the unsettling nature of water. She renders narratives surrounding water's role both as a physical and a metaphorical force (p. 32).

These contributions are followed by inquiries into agricultural water management practices: Stefan Breit and Jelena Streit discuss the historical significance and contemporary challenges of a water storage and irrigation system in the Mediterranean (p. 38). Elanz Najar Najafi and Negar Sanaan Bensi draw our attention to water harvesting techniques that emerged in a desert environment structured by 'thirst,' revealing how this notion becomes generative for maintaining arid landscapes (p. 50). The essays that follow delve into themes of fluidity and transformation, highlighting the dynamic interplay between human constructs and natural forces in defining spaces: while Stavroula Michael focuses on the colonial and post-colonial water infrastructure of Cyprus, emphasizing systemic inequalities and the role of women in shaping water narratives (p. 58), Lucia Rebolino and Federica Pessotto explore the fluidity of borders from a geopolitical perspective through captivating digital representations underscoring water's role in continually reshaping boundaries (p. 66).

The two final essays of the issue address the challenges associated with the infrastructures of industrial water management. Linda Schilling Cuellar critiques the technological and privatization aspects of desalination in Chile amidst the climate crisis (p. 74), and Oskar Frederick Johanson uses the sonic environment of Warragamba Dam in Australia to explore complexities of water harvesting against a backdrop of colonial history and environmental concerns (p. 82).

5 Erik Swyngedouw, *Social Power and the Urbanization of Water: Flows of Power* (Oxford: Oxford University Press, 2004), cited in Matthew Gandy, "Rethinking Urban Metabolism: Water, Space and the Modern City," *City* 8, no. 3 (2004): 363.

6 Ursula K. Le Guin, "119. The Election, Lao Tzu, a Cup of Water," *Ursula K. Le Guin* (blog), n.d. ursulakleguin.com/blog/119-the-electionlao-tzu-a-cup-of-water.

A glacier, a dam, a navel. I gaze into my own navel, which expands to the infinite loops of life and death, both natural and human-made. Navel-gazing, deriving from the Greek words ὀμφᾰλός [navel] and σκέψῐς [speculation], refers to the act of using one's own navel to contemplate the cosmos. However, if viewed in excess, the gazing can lead to self-absorbed, narcissistic pursuits. Like the building of a reservoir, navel-gazing involves considering the source of life – a glacier, the navel – and treads a fragile balance between renewal and destruction. I use the dying glacier, the artificial lake and the rivers that flow out of them to contemplate our future co-existence with nature, constantly teetering on the edge between life and death, good and bad, past and future. These opposites are manifested through the visual tension between concrete and earth.

Yumna
Al-Arashi

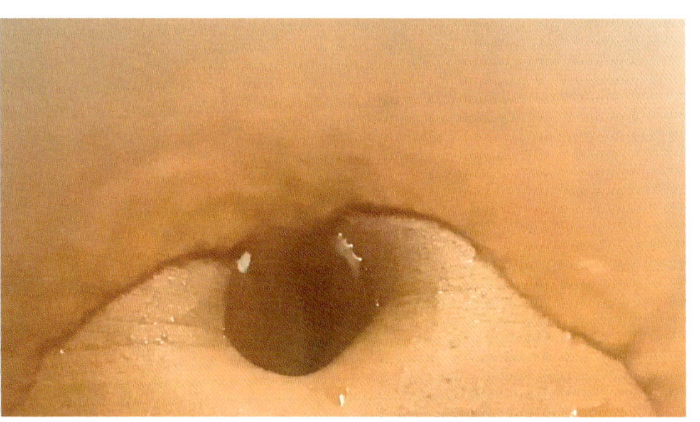

All images by the author, 2023.

Navel Gazing

Yumna
Al-Arashi

The Draining of the Fens: Enclosures, Resistance and Wilderness

Mathilde Redouté traces the evolution of England's Fens from a waterlogged marshland to drained, arable land. Water takes centre stage in this tale, positioned between wasteland and wilderness and set against a backdrop of local resistance. While some sought to rid themselves of its presence, others recognized its potential and defended it as their ultimate sanctuary.

Covering over 1 300 square miles – twice the size of London – England's Fens are unique in their nature and history. Characterized as an undetermined marsh, the Fens challenge the neatly classifiable and productive vision of the landscape. The sixteenth-century enclosure movement, aimed at 'improving' England's economic landscape, reached the Fens and their inhabitants, both of which were quickly portrayed as 'waste' in need of civilizing by emerging external actors such as the Adventurers, the Projectors and prominent landowners. These actors collaborated closely with the Crown in reimagining the nation as a clean and picturesque state. The proposed drainage projects for the Fens were social as much as they were spatial endeavours, designed to dry up any ungoverned wilderness. Comprising "the largest group of English people still to be brought under effective state, ecclesiastical, landlord, and employer control,"[1] the Fenland's inhabitants fiercely fought for their territory and way of life for over 250 years, marking their opposition as one of the most important English resistance movements.

Over time, the marshy and impenetrable land and its inhabitants were eventually subjected to the logic of geometry, abstraction and surplus production. The unique culture of the Fenland, which relied on water management for refuge, vanished along with this transformation. This essay explores the multifaceted history of the Fens, revisiting the ecological impact of transforming a fluid landscape into arable land and highlighting the socio-political conflicts resulting from local resistance against the enclosure movements. By juxtaposing the Fens' natural mutability against human attempts to impose order and productivity, this essay reveals how these interventions reshaped both the land and its inhabitants.

For centuries, the Fenland's geography was directly connected to the weather – storms, high tides and wind. Some areas were under water in winter but dry in summer, while others were permanently flooded. Over eras of continuous but rhythmic alterations, this basin gradually silted up through a combination of deposits from the upland rivers and the sea itself.

Mathilde Redouté

1 James Boyce, *Imperial Mud: The Fight for the Fens* (London: Icon Books, 2020).

1607.

A true report of certaine wonderfull ouerflowings of Waters, now lately in Summerſet-ſhire, Norfolke, and other places of England: deſtroying many thouſands of men, women, and children, ouerthrowing and bearing downe whole townes and villages, and drowning infinite numbers of ſheepe and other Cattle.

Printed at London by W. I. for Edward White and are to be ſolde at the ſigne of the Gunne at the North doore of Paules.

A

"A true report of certaine wonderfull overflowing of Waters, now lately in Summerset-shire, Norfolke, and other places of England," London, 1607. British Library.

The soil was uneven – sometimes a mix of silt and clay deposit, sometimes peat, formed by the extended coexistence of stagnant waters and decomposed vegetation. This landscape hosted numerous occasional or stable hills, perceived as islands, upon which the region's earliest permanent settlements were located. Mutability and instability were the territory's defining characteristics. In the midst of this environment, inhabitants were at the mercy of the waters. Great floods could drown an entire village, as they did in Somerset and Norfolk in 1607 (**FIG. A**). In this context, roads were impossible to build or maintain permanently. In Vittoria Di Palma's words:

> The isolation and desolation of Fenland, together with the changeable characteristics of its watery landscape, resulted in the development of a unique culture, separate and distinct from the rest of the country, with firm division between insiders and outsiders.[2]

The occasional visitors began to picture this ecosystem as a barren backwater, associated with a putrid smell, disease and danger. The characterization of the Fens as wasteland and its inhabitants as both insulated and ignorant can be found in some of the earliest descriptions of the medieval landscape. As professor of medieval archaeology Susan Oosthuizen demonstrates, when the Germanic tribes arrived in Britain, fens had long been used by Britons, who would have modelled some uses of the environment, as evidenced by sites such as Flag Fen, with its wooden roadways. In the centuries after 400 CE, the local Saxon population of the time, known as the *Gyrwe*, steadily increased.[3] This name, which later evolved into *Girvii*, referred to the people of the mud/marsh:[4]

> A sort of people (much like the place) of British uncivilized tempers, envious of all others, whom they term Upland-men, and usually walking aloft upon a sort of stilts: they keep to the business of grazing, fishing and fowling.[5]

The Fens were often depicted as "manifold horrors," as suggested by Felix of Crowland in his *Life of St. Guthlac,*[6] inhabited only by "bands of outlaws and solitary hermits," and Fennish people were constantly vilified by outsiders (**FIG. B**). As reported by an anonymous traveller in 1635:

> I think they be half-fish, half-flesh, for they drink like fishes, & sleep like hogs ... Their climate is so infinitely old, & watery; their habitations so poor, and mean; their means so small, & scant; their diet so course and sluttish; & their bodies so lazy, and intemperate.[7]

They were directly identified and associated with their land, which was both a source of disdain and envy.

As Susan Oosthuizen shows, by 1334, the Fennish basin was among the wealthiest and most populated regions in England.[8] Fish, eels, waterfowl, corn grown in gardens and dairy from extended grazed livestock provided enough food to survive during the year. Fennish houses were constructed with wattle and daub, featuring latticed wooden walls clagged together with a mixture of soil, clay and straw, roofed with reeds, insulated with abundant sheep's wool, deerskin and bird feathers, and heated with peat.[9] Resources were abundant, and the land was fertile and accessible thanks to the inhabitants' deep understanding of and intimate relationship with the ecosystem. During the flooding season, they would navigate on stilts, vault over dykes with poles or ice skate over the frozen areas. Rather than an anarchic "wide wilderness," as the great historical geographer Clifford Darby called it, the Fens were governed by careful and complex intercommoning.

These practices were based on a specific semi-nomadic system that had ensured ecological and economic stability for thousands of years, through inter-village negotiations, specific group allotments, seasonal restriction and, if needed, the use of local courts for sanctions. In 1882, English surveyor J. S. Padley wrote:

> Every person having a right in this Fen, had the privilege of employing two labourers, and with them, would go down into the Fen on the evening before Midsummer Day, and lie down until they heard the report of a gun which was fired exactly at twelve o'clock (midnight); then each party would arise and set to work.
> By common agreement, all the 'fodder' they could mow path around became the frontager's own property.[10]

These customary laws were respected by everyone to ensure the preservation of resources and well-being of all through active cooperation over the year.

The traditional economy and ecology of commoning were nonetheless subject to the constant flux of changes. A cooling climate during the Little Ice Age, coupled with rising seas and less stable rivers, made the Fens ever more flood-prone. By the mid-thirteenth century, precisely during the period when these changes were occurring, the Crown began to take a much greater interest in wetland customs for maintaining local drainage. This was evidenced by the issuance of sewer commissions to better understand and control the territory. But beyond the ecological and geographical changes, a series of socio-economic developments placed additional strain on the region. Inspired by the 'enclosure movement' already taking place in the rest of the country, and following Henry VIII's dissolution of the many large monasteries that previously dominated the Fennish landscape, the pattern of land ownership in the Fens began to undergo significant disruption.[11] By 1540, the confusion was total, with the influx of several new landlords from outside the Fens paired with a rising population due to the increase of landless in-migrants from other parts of the country. Together, these conditions placed unprecedented pressure on the available commons. "The complicated customary systems of intercommoning between Fenland communities were breaking down, as scarcity prompted neighbouring villages to challenge one another's use rights within a shared fen."[12] In addition, these newcomers, to whom the traditional economy seemed "alien" and "irrational," overstocked the commons, turning them into waste (**FIG. C**). Together, these circumstances created an opening for forces outside the Fens (the centralizing monarchical state, the projectors who served it and the investors who backed them) to intervene, on the promise of immense rewards for draining and ploughing the land for grain.

These outsiders brought with them a radical new understanding of the Fenland environment and an alternative model for its optimal management and exploitation. The re-imagined project for the 'improvement' of the Fens was launched in the early 1600s by Charles I and the Earl of Bedford. Lacking expertise for a project of this magnitude in England, they turned to Dutch engineers, notably Cornelius Vermuyden, who was employed to undertake comprehensive drainage schemes. To finance the project, the Crown promised to allocate a third of the land enclosed and drained to the new developers; this system had the advantage of not requiring funds from the Crown's own coffers and of keeping the investors motivated to complete the work.[13] The whole transformation was planned in London by engineers and wealthy external landowners, minimizing their on-site presence as much as possible.

2 Vittoria Di Palma, "Swamp," in *Wasteland: A History* (New Haven and London: Yale University Press, 2014), 88.

3 Susan Oosthuizen, *The Anglo-Saxon Fenland* (Bollington: Windgather Press, 2017), 21.

4 Kelley M. Wickham-Crowley, "Fens and Frontiers," in *Water and the Environment in the Anglo-Saxons World,* ed. Maren Clegg Hyer and Della Hooke (Liverpool: Liverpool University Press, 2017), 68.

5 William Camden, *Britannia* (1971), 408–9.

6 Bertram Colgrave, ed., *Felix's Life of Saint Guthlac: Texts, Translation and Notes* (Cambridge, UK: Cambridge University Press, 1985).

7 Greg Frey, "A Tale of Web-Toed Tigers," *The Land: Wetter and Wilder?* 32 (2023): 28.

8 Oosthuizen, *The Anglo-Saxon Fenland* (see note 3), 14.

9 Frey, "A Tale of Web-Toed Tigers" (see note 7): 28.

10 James Sandby Padley, *The Fens and Floods of Mid-Lincolnshire with a Description of the River Witham and Its Improvements Up to 1825* (Lincoln: C. Akrill High Street and Silver Street, 1882).

11 Eric H. Ash, *The Draining of the Fens: Projectors, Popular Politics,*

Mathilde Redouté

Ironically, the participants struggled to forge a consensus due to lack of trust, having brought in a Dutch engineer – an outsider – to manage and transform 'their' territory. After years of discussion, they finally launched the project, which unfolded in two phases. The first great level drainage was carried out from 1630 to 1642, but was interrupted by riots and the civil war (1642–1651). The second great level drainage was completed in 1656. To conquer, or colonize, their own country, the 'Adventurers,' as this group called themselves, relied heavily on mathematics and cartographic skills. It was their way of reassuring English viewers, "discerning order from the topographic confusion" and "imposing a civilized regularity on the land."[14]

Towards the end of the conversion of water to land, the Adventurers commissioned William Dugdale, a well-known antiquarian, to showcase the triumph of the drainage project. Along with a book, he produced two maps of the territory: one that was supposed to illustrate the Fens before and one after the 'improvement.' The first is dominated by a massive pool of shadows, as if the whole territory had been covered with water, suggesting that it was all one massive quagmire (**FIG. D**). There is almost nothing about the land depicted in this map that looks man-made, or even inhabitable; it is a region over which capricious nature has full sway, uncontrolled and apparently uncontrollable.[15] The second, post-drainage map was meant to portray the establishment of order and reason on a wild, unpredictable and unprofitable water (**FIG. E**). Dugdale used the idea of geometry to display order and productivity, "as well as beauty and virtue."[16] Both maps successfully conveyed the triumph of human reason, persistence, labour and civilization over the disordered tyranny of unruly nature and people.

The project to transform the Fens was not only about the wetland but also about the people. Described as lazy, dangerous and selfish for not exploiting their territory to its maximum, the Fenland's inhabitants were subjected to vilification by outsiders. They were portrayed as backward, brutish people. The Adventurers' goal was to transform (or replace) them so they would no longer "be suffered to lead idle, unproductive, disreputable lives but would become honest, hardworking, civilized farmers."[17] But the Fennish people did not let the project proceed without opposition. Local resistance was intense and widespread. Led by small groups of women, resistance to new enclosures was the strongest in the country. For 250 years, villagers formed alliances, fought the Adventurers, sabotaged and levelled the ditches they built, organized riots and even took the engineers to court. In 1646, an anonymous pamphlet titled "The Anti-Projector" was circulated to counter the growing influence of the Projector, a figure associated with the Adventurers. This individual was described as "both entrepreneurial and public spirited, whose schemes promised to combine private profit with public benefit,"[18] frequently promoting expansive industrial initiatives on a large scale:[19]

> The Undertakers [Projectors] have alwaies vilified the fens, and have misinformed many Parliament men, that all the fens is a meer quagmire, and that it is a level hurtfully surrounded and of little or no value: but those who live in the fens and are neighbours to it, know the contrary.[20]

Their efforts were not in vain. In 1645, all the drainers' banks in the Isle of Axholme were destroyed. And between 1642 and 1649, the Crown's share of Fenland in numerous parishes was seized by the inhabitants and returned to the commons. After the civil war, however, the drainers returned and sought to seize back most of the land, this time more successfully. The Adventurers were favoured by the high price of crops and the decline

and State Building in Early Modern England (Baltimore: Johns Hopkins University Press, 2017); James Boyce, *Imperial Mud* (see note 1).

12 Ash, *The Draining of the Fens* (see note 11), 49.

13 Simon Fairlie, "A Short History of Enclosures in Britain," *The Land* 7 (Summer 2009).

14 Ash, *The Draining of the Fens* (see note 11), 290.

15 Ash, *The Draining of the Fens* (see note 11), 296.

16 Ash, *The Draining of the Fens* (see note 11), 291.

17 Ash, *The Draining of the Fens* (see note 11), 296.

18 Michael Zell, "Walter Morrell and the New Draperies Project, *c.* 1603–1631," *The Historical Journal* 44, no. 3 (2001): 652.

19 Alex Keller, "The Age of the Projectors," *History Today* 16, no. 7 (1966): 467–74.

20 *The Anti-projector, or, The History of the Fen Project* (s.l.: s.n., Early English Book Online EEBO 1646).

LEFT
Map of Cambridge and the Isle of Ely, Engraved by William Hole for *Drayton's Poly Olbion*, 1622. British Library.

of solidarity amongst commoners. Wealthier Adventurers exacerbated the new, unstable situation by overstocking the commons with their animals over winter.[21] As a result, between 1760 and 1840 most of the Fens were drained and enclosed with the support of parliament. But their objectives were only partially attained: as the land dried out, it shrank and lowered against the water table – and so became even more vulnerable to flooding. Pumping stations had to be introduced, and even today the entire area is kept dry by diesel machines.

In addition to these structural consequences, the transformations led to the flooding of adjacent territories, still inhabited by commoners who were helpless against this new form of invasion. One recalled: "Their horses go lame, children take ill, lambs die and houses fall apart."[22] By changing the nature of the soil, the Adventurers alienated the protective spirit of the Fens. In fact, during the seventeenth and eighteenth centuries, large landowners, projectors and enterprising investors worked hand in hand with the Crown to transform England's Fens, even providing legal power and military labour (sometimes in the form of imported prisoners of war) to support the venture against the many claims and riots of the people to defend and care for their territory.

The example of the Fens is significant, as it played a role in establishing 'wasteland' as the dichotomous counterpart to 'wilderness,' signifying a shift in social and economic perspectives. While the two terms have been used interchangeably in the past, by the end of the eighteenth century, wilderness came to describe uncultivated but controlled and designed land. Evoking sublime sentiments of order, it became the nemesis of wasteland, which was defined as messy and spoiled by inefficient human use. This paradigmatic change, based on the surplus accumulation that a landscape would produce and associated with the centralization of territory management, created a potential – and need – for a new aesthetic: the picturesque. Literally translated as 'fit to be made into a picture,' this new landscape ideal was labelled as beautiful and sublime. Its opposite – more difficult to understand, capture and control from the outside, like the Fens – was considered repugnant and dangerous. This spatial and social division created fertile ground for an internal colonization strategy. By categorizing landscape based on its visual appeal, it birthed the concept of the 'Other' – the "radically different, and hence incorrigibly inferior."[23] This "rule of colonial difference," as Partha Chatterjee phrases it, brings forth its unique mode of representation and discourse, applicable to both individuals and natural entities, whether within or beyond imperial borders. The practice of internal enclosures occurred at the same time as English colonial interventions elsewhere and can be viewed as an integral component of its broader system, revealing new connections within its interconnected spheres of operation.[24]

To conclude, the Fens emerge as a microcosm of the broader tensions between nature and civilization, tradition and progress. Their transformation from a semi-nomadic haven to drained, arable land reflects broader societal shifts in values and priorities. Many outsiders invested great fortunes, hoping to reap even greater rewards, but ended up slinking away "without faithful performance of what they promise ... with more knowledge and less money."[25] As history professor Eric H. Ash demonstrates: in spite of the enormous difficulty and expense, the Adventurers and the Crown still 'succeeded' little by little, for a time, in transforming the region into fertile farmland, only to see their labour and investment dry up and blow away, like the desiccated peat they had bought so dearly. In this muddy fight, Fennish radicalism ended up dying with the last of England's large copper butterflies as the drainage of the last remaining wetland was taking place in 1840.

"They (the Fenland people) had to tell themselves that, for the first time since the Fens were made, those living in them were beaten."[26] The Fens' status as an enclave and refuge for dissidence was at an end. Because drainage eventually transformed the area into one of the most productive regions of arable farmland in Britain, it would be difficult to argue that it was not an economic improvement. However, this transformation was bought with social and environmental consequences. The Fennish tale unfolds here, not in mere reclamation, but as a testament to the nuanced relationship between water and land, as a vision born and cradled in the embrace of existence. With so much labour, money and energy expended to reimagine the landscape as drained, arable farmland, it is somehow ironic that today, organizations such as the Royal Society for the Protection of Birds (RSPB), the Wildfowl & Wetlands Trust (WWT) and the National Trust are working so hard to 'rewild' them as wetland reserves by pumping water back into them … As the Fennish author Greg Frey puts it:

> This is the awkward way in which, the colonial tale of a dull, blank landscape in need of civilizing became a self-fulfilling prophecy. Decolonization, now, in this particular place, requires reviving the alternative radical history, remembering the abundance lost and noticing what survives.[27]

Between wasteland and wilderness, the history of the Fens ultimately revolves around water: some sought to dispose of it, while others, recognizing its potential, pursued it as their ultimate sanctuary. •

21 Joan Thirsk, quoted in Fairlie, "A Short History of Enclosures in Britain" (see note 13).

22 Frey, "A Tale of Web-Toed Tigers" (see note 7): 28.

23 Partha Chatterjee, *The Nation and Its Fragments: Colonial and Postcolonial Histories* (Princeton, NJ: Princeton University Press, 1994).

24 Hollyamber Kennedy, "Infrastructures of 'Legitimate Violence': The Prussian Settlement Commission, Internal Colonization, and the Migrant Remainder," *Grey Room* 76 (September 2019).

25 Anonymous letter to an unknown recipient, NA, SPD 14/128/105 (n.d. [*c.* 1619–20]).

26 W. H. Barrett, *Tales from the Fens,* ed. Enid Porter (London: The Country Book Club and Routledge & Kegan Paul; Book Club Edition, 1966).

27 Frey, "A Tale of Web-Toed Tigers" (see note 7): 30.

C

"Aliens, or a Mixed Crew: A Study in the Fen Country," Robert Walker Macbeth RA, (1848–1910).

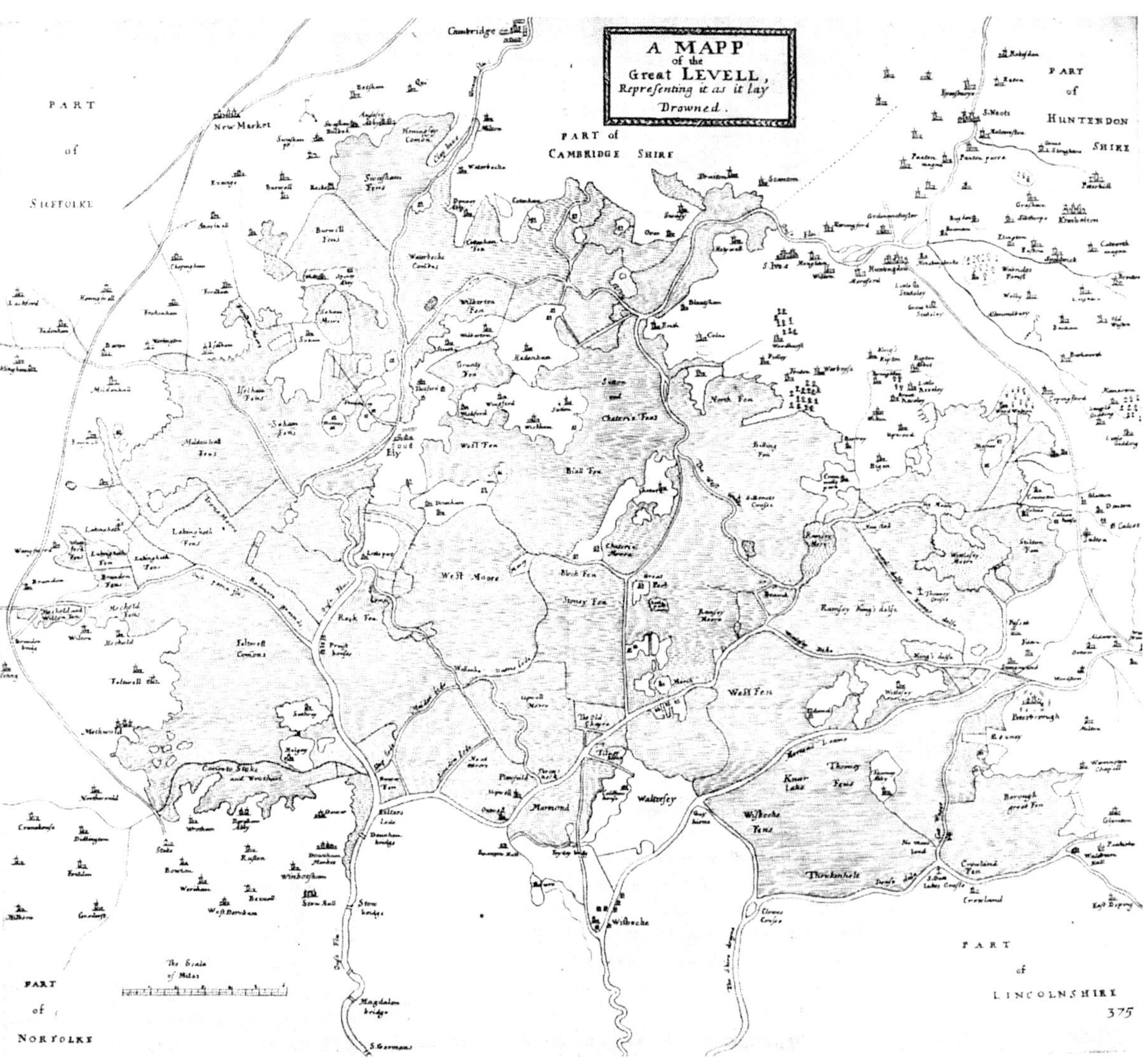
A MAPP
of the
Great LEVELL,
Representing it as it lay
Drowned.
PART of
CAMBRIDGE SHIRE
PART
of
SUFFOLKE
PART
of
HUNTERDON
SHIRE
PART
of
LINCOLNSHIRE
PART
of
NORFOLKE
Cambridge
New Market
Ely
West Moore
Stoney Fen
Bliss Fen
West Fen
Wisbeche
Peterborough
Crowland
The Scale
of Miles
375

D E

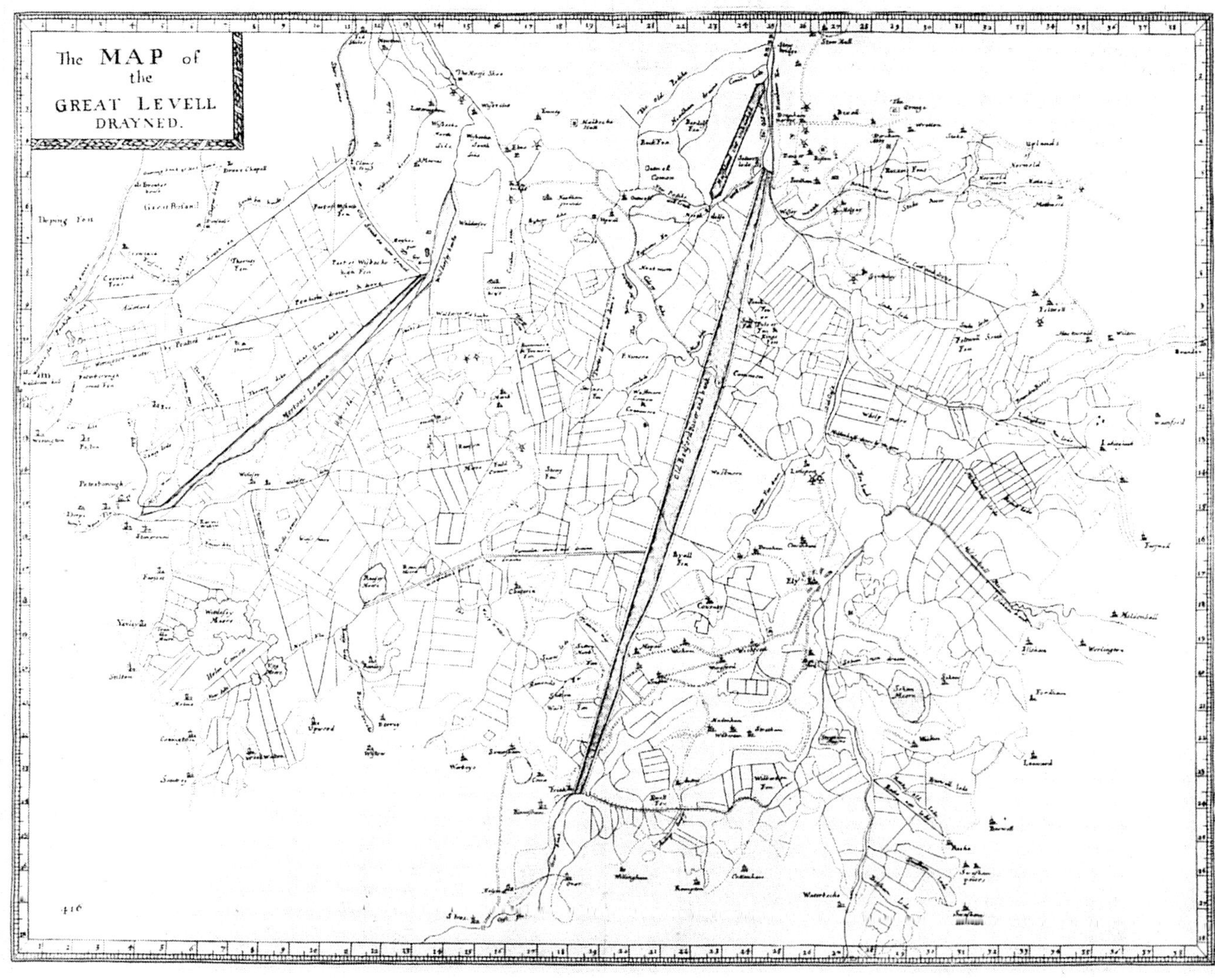

D "A Mapp of the Great Levell, Representing it as it lay Drowned," *The History of Imbanking and Drayning of Divers Fenns and Marshes* (London, 1662). The William Andrew Clark Memorial Library.

E "The Map of the Great Levell Drayned," *The History of Imbanking and Drayning of Divers Fenns and Marshes* (London, 1662). The William Andrew Clark Memorial Library.

Embroidered Waterscapes: Unpacking Relationships through Artisanal Map-making

Akshar Gajjar and Bhavya Jain urge us to behold a nineteenth-century pashmina shawl, a masterpiece intricately charting Srinagar's waterways. They juxtapose artisanal insight and colonial mapping, advocating an embroidered ethos. Through threads and layered textiles, they defy the hegemony of Cartesian water cartography.

Akshar Gajjar,
Bhavya Jain

In the late 1800s, the king of the princely state of Jammu and Kashmir commissioned the city's pashmina shawl weavers to represent the capital city of Srinagar cartographically in four shawls. Today, two of these shawls are in the possession of the Victoria and Albert Museum in London – with one of these being on loan from the Royal Collections (**FIG. A**). Another shawl can be found in the National Gallery of Australia, while another is held by the Sri Pratap Singh Museum in Srinagar itself. These shawls provide a snapshot of the city's essence: frozen in time and perspective, they offer a window into the period in which they were embroidered, the purpose behind their creation and their intended recipients, who were either foreign traders or colonial royalty. The shawls represent the city through the lens of weavers and embroiderers, revealing the socio-economic context of the artisans who made pashmina shawls and encapsulating the city's unique biodiversity, architecture and culture. We begin this essay with an inquiry into one of these cartographic masterpieces, exploring how water, in interaction with the city and the land, was seen and understood by its artisans. Was water confined within the boundaries of the land or depicted as an integral part of artistic expression? Did ecological features take a leading role in the representation, or were they merely secondary to the built form of the city? Secondly, we compare the artisanal representation of water and land in the embroidered and woven map shawl with the colonial trigonometric survey map of Kashmir, which captures industrial perceptions and representations of water and water bodies. We argue that colonial and post-colonial map-making exercises have been a project of progress and longevity in which fragility is undesirable. By linking and comparing the socio-ecological cultures of Srinagar and their representation (or lack thereof) in artisanal and colonial map-making practices, we propose the possibility of and need for an alternate paradigm of representing cities that is cognizant of the flexibility and fragility of water as an element that co-exists with landscape and built forms. In the final section of this essay, we synthesize our investigations by presenting a tapestry we embroidered in response to the intricate and diverse artisanal

RIGHT
Woven and embroidered Kashmiri map shawl. London, Victoria and Albert Museum, South & South East Asia Collections, Gift of Mrs Estelle Fuller through The Art Fund, IS.31-1970.

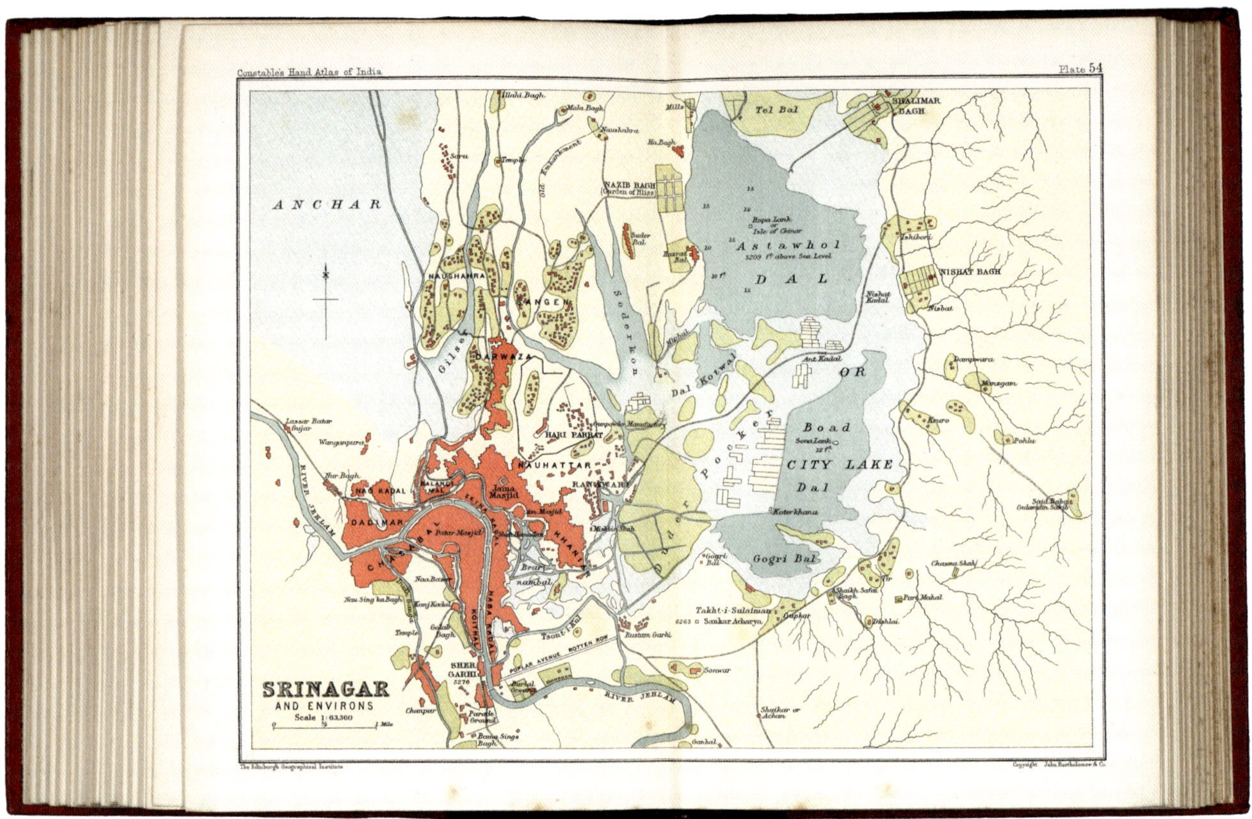
Constable's Hand Atlas of India
Plate 54
SRINAGAR
AND ENVIRONS
Scale 1:63,360
ANCHAR
Astawhol
DAL
CITY LAKE
Boad
Dal
OR
Tel Bal
Gogri Bal
SHALIMAR BAGH
NISHAT BAGH
NAZIB BAGH
Garden of Bliss
NAUSHAHRA
SANGEN
DARWAZA
HARI PARBAT
NAUHATTAR
RANAWARI
NAO KADAL
DADIMAR
Jama Masjid
SHER GARHI
5276
RIVER JEHLAM
POPLAR AVENUE ROTTEN ROW
Takht-i-Sulaiman
6263 Sankar Acharya
Dal Kotwal
Soderkon
Gilsar
5209 ft above Sea Level
Ropa Lank or Isle of Chinar
Ilahi Bagh
Mala Bagh
Naushahra
Temple
Sara
Suder Bal
Nishat
Nishat Kadal
Ishibari
Dampwara
Manzgan
Pohlu
Chasma Shahi
Pari Mahal
Shaikh Safai Bagh
Koterkhana
Gogri Bal
Nau Bazar
Temple
Gulab Bagh
Chanpur
Sonwar
Shalkar or Achan
Gunbal
Nur Bagh
Wangapura
Lassar Batar Gujar
Mission Shah
Rustam Garhi
Tsont-i-Kol
The Edinburgh Geographical Institute
Copyright. John Bartholomew & Co.

practices encountered here. This allows for an experienced and embodied account of the process of embroidering a map.

THE MAP SHAWL AND THE TRIGONOMETRIC SURVEY: PARALLEL HISTORIES

The pashmina shawl industry reached its economic peak in the late sixteenth century, with the incorporation of the region within the Mughal Empire. Since then, the importance of the shawl as an object of trade increased, while the techniques of the craft continued evolving with influences from changing dynasties and knowledge exchange through trade. The map shawls were commissioned in the third quarter of the nineteenth century by the Dogra King Maharaja Ranbir Singh of Jammu and Kashmir. During this period, the shawl industry was a streamlined, revenue-generating state asset that needed a boost in order to compete with French imitation shawl-making techniques.[1]

The industry and its artisans were scrutinized by the state, and the craft was systematized through taxation systems that were often met with resistance by the craftspeople. Never intended to be worn, the elaborate map shawls are a combination of embroidery and weaving. They were commissioned to establish a powerful position for the kingdom and its suzerainty through the means of artisanship – representing a product of a self-sufficient, local industry and knowledge system.[2] Around the same time, between 1855 and 1865, the region of Kashmir was mapped under the Grand Trigonometric Survey of India, an imperial endeavour aimed at surveying the subcontinent and ultimately turning it into a finite, measurable entity **(FIG. B)**. Hence, the commission of local map shawls can also be explained as a response to colonial practices of map-making that had reached the region concurrently.

Cartography and surveys were necessary for the British economic system to establish itself in the territory, which had not been incorporated into colonial rule.[3] This led to a period of negotiation and consolidation of power between both the political entities in the region – the Dogra rulers and the Empire. This political context allows us to read the making of the map shawls as a symbolic process. Commissioned by local rulers, the shawls represent the kingdom as a sum of its parts: the city, artisans, rulers and their combined contextual knowledge (of cultural diversity and biodiversity) on a par with, if not superior to British knowledge and governance systems. Though meant to be imperial gifts, the map shawls contend the imposition of a colonial mapping rationale by asserting a local comprehension of the city, as opposed to the methods of the trigonometric survey, which required mathematical precision in plotting a landscape.[4] Both the process of shawl making and the final product foreground a tacit knowledge of land, water and the built environment as opposed to the trigonometrically measured map, which – in its abstract form – is devoid of a lived and intimate cultural, social and ecological understanding of the city.[5]

MAP SHAWLS: UNPACKING THE MULTIPLICITIES

The shawls offer a 150-year-old, multi-perspectival comprehension of geography. Reading these maps against the backdrop of the trigonometric survey enables an alternate understanding of territorial relationships, which in turn allows for the debunking of some of the most common myths of land-water relationships in modern Euro-American representation. The diversity and variety in the representation of the city exemplify a plural understanding of its natural and built features. As Graham Huggan has argued, the multiplicity of perceptions of a city reflects the interplay between the control exerted over the map-making process and the freedom granted to the map maker.[6] It is fair to assume

1 Frank Ames, "Classification of the Kashmir Shawl," in *The Kashmir Shawl and Its Indo-French Influence*, 3rd ed. (Woodbridge: Antique Collectors' Club, 1997), 15–52.

2 Paul Sharrad, "Following the Map: A Postcolonial Unpacking of a Kashmir Shawl," *Textile: The Journal of Cloth and Culture* 2, no. 1 (March 2004): 64–78.

3 Miguel Ohnesorge, "Theodolites at 20 000 Feet: Justifying Precision Measurement during the Trigonometrical Survey of Kashmir, 1855–1865," *Notes and Records of the Royal Society of London* 76, no. 3 (February 17, 2021): 603–18.

4 Dilip da Cunha, "River of Rivers," in *Invention of Rivers: Alexander's Eye and Ganga's Descent*, Penn Studies in Landscape Architecture (Philadelphia: University of Pennsylvania Press, 2019), 45–74.

5 Sharrad, "Following the Map" (see note 2).

B

LEFT
John George Bartholomew, 1860–1920, "Srinagar and its Environs," Plate 54, *Constable's Hand Atlas of India*. David Rumsey Historical Map Collection, David Rumsey Map Center, Stanford Libraries.

that the complex palimpsests and stories woven and embroidered in the map shawls are an outcome of an acknowledgement of these multiple perceptions of the city and the freedom to represent a particular perception. These maps, therefore, do not claim to be complete or absolute. They constitute an agglomeration of the lenses through which the city was seen by weavers and embroiderers at the time. They are artefacts of local knowledge and carry a rich understanding of a place by people with lived experience.

The artisanal expressions found in the map shawl of Srinagar at the Victoria and Albert Museum[7] (**FIG. A**) vividly portray topographical, ecological and built features. These include humans, flora and fauna, rituals, festivals and so on, and highlight the land-water-built nexus. This interconnectedness is expressed in a variety of ways, showing complex and multiple land-water edge conditions. Moreover, the embroidered map conveys an ephemeral quality that contrasts starkly with the search for accuracy embodied by trigonometric mapping techniques and depicts the more transitory nature of a city permeated by lakes and the Jhelum River. Here, the landscape can be understood as an agglomeration of the basins of Dal Lake, the marshy lands on its banks, islands, and inhabited lands that interweave with the waters in a gradual transition. This unique landscape is dotted with vernacular rural settlements, colonial houseboats, traditional floating irrigation systems, gardens, fountains, monuments and many other layers of building and rebuilding. While embodying this geography, the map shawl ensures that several characteristics of water are evidenced (beyond its mere presence). These features are highlighted in the next sections.

WATER IS NOT FORGOTTEN

If cartography is a political technology of world-making, then the intricacy with which it carries information becomes pertinent to decisions taken during building practices.[8] Water, represented in a light shade of blue, has a sharp presence throughout the map shawl. It is not forgotten – even in the most intricate corners. This creates a comprehensive picture of the city's water system, highlighting many of its infrastructures and natural conditions. The shade of blue connects the river with the lake, the lake with the artificial tanks, the canals, the irrigation system of floating gardens, ponds in the city and even the source of water. The representation becomes a cartographic document carrying information about ecological and infrastructural water flows in the city and foregrounds this relation with respect to the socio-spatial functioning of the rest of the city.

WATER IS NEVER EMPTY

When looking at the water in the shawl, one sees it as 'full': birds, animals, humans and houseboats are depicted throughout the water system. This contrasts with colonial maps of India produced at the same time, which show 'empty' water, devoid of any information about its riverine ecosystem and biodiversity (**FIG. B**). Within the map shawl, both artificial and natural edge conditions are uniquely interwoven with flora and fauna, clearly expressing ecological diversity across different conditions. The artificial water outlet from the built complex is lined with trimmed and maintained trees, while the marshy lands host different kinds of shrubs. The water is covered with different varieties and densities of weeds that change with land conditions and human intervention. There is a concentration of weeds on the edge of marshy lands and a sparsity of weeds next to the built levees – exemplary of the embroiderers' specificity in representation and eye for detail.

WATER AS AN OVERLAPPING SPACE

In an attempt to capture human life, the map shawl represents water as an essential part of the human geography of the region.

It intermingles with the economic order, where trade, power and worship exist alongside humans, fish, plants and animals. In the process, the mechanisms of living next to water are also foregrounded. The boats on the lake are shown in all their diversity, representing the myriad of actors in an economic system of floating boats selling fruit and houseboat shops as they relate to the water bodies. One can observe boat people cleaning the weeds with broom-like oars next to royal boats – displayed in all their glory and most likely harbouring important members of society onboard. This floating economy of Srinagar is a consequence of its geography of islets and marshes, which often change forms.[9] People adapt to these changing forms through maintenance procedures. Thus, the relationship between people and nature is important to capturing the essence of how landscapes and waterscapes exist in everyday life. This cultural richness is, therefore, an important indicator of the physicality of land-water.

WATER BEYOND ITS PLANAR REPRESENTATION

The map shawl does not conform to the planar, Cartesian interpretation of landscapes. Cartography merges plan, elevations, sections and sometimes even axonometric forms, a representational technique also popular in other art forms of that time and region.[10] Sections and other representative forms that go beyond the surveyor's birds-eye view express a sense of depth that is critical to the relationship between land and water. This makes it possible to record sequences and rhythms between water and land, incorporating fluidity as part of a static representation.[11] In turn, this contends the line, which is an artefact of linear thinking, a binary abstraction of water and land with edges dotted with diverse interactions. The map shawl demonstrates the meaningfulness of artisanal thinking in representing land-water-human relationships. While being a form of art, these shawls also lend themselves to a deeper understanding of natural and cultural ecosystems of water bodies in Srinagar – their source, body, edges and interactions with different entities: human and non-human, physical and ephemeral.

LANDSCAPE EMBROIDERY: REDEFINING PROCESSES AND REPRESENTATIONS OF WATERSCAPES

To respond to the woven and embroidered map of Kashmir with words alone feels distant and incomplete. While the visual aspects of this work provide insights into the relationship between human and non-human entities, it is important not to read these in isolation from embroidery as a process and tool for representation. Therefore, we ask: Where does the use of embroidery lead? How does the process change our perception of the landscape? To investigate, we embroidered a tapestry that synthesizes some of our learnings and observations (**FIG. C**). Our piece is in no way an emulation of the Kashmiri map shawl. Firstly, ours is not Kashmiri style, as it draws from the Gujarati embroidery style taught to Akshar (one of the two authors) by his mother.[12] Furthermore, the Kashmiri map shawl took thirty years to complete; ours is a reflection on the time, energy and effort that goes into this process. Finally, the elements featured in our map do not represent a particular geography, but rather a visualization of our understanding of the fluidity of the land-water nexus and the various elements that constitute this fluidity.

The tapestry-making process began with patching and overlapping various fabrics – analogous to stitching together different landscape types. In contrast to a map on paper with uniform thickness, the variably thick fabrics offer a three-dimensional, tactile understanding of the territory. To hold these thicknesses while embroidering creates a unique physical engagement with the territory.

6 Graham Huggan, "Decolonizing the Map: Postcolonialism, Poststructuralism and the Cartographic Connection," *Interdisciplinary Measures: Literature and the Future of Postcolonial Studies* (Liverpool: Liverpool University Press, 2008), 21–33.

7 London, Victoria and Albert Museum, South & South East Asia Collections, Gift of Mrs Estelle Fuller through The Art Fund, IS.31-1970.

8 Reuben Rose-Redwood, Natchee Blu Barnd, Annita Hetoevėhotohke'e Lucchesi, Sharon Dias and Wil Patrick, "Decolonizing the Map: Recentering Indigenous Mappings," *Cartographica: The International Journal for Geographic Information and Geovisualization* 55, no. 3 (2020): 151–62.

9 Michael J. Casimir, *Floating Economies: The Cultural Ecology of the Dal Lake in Kashmir, India* (New York: Berghahn, 2021).

10 Miniature paintings in Mughal traditions are well known for such representations. The use of such a technique in the map shawls can be attributed to their influence.

11 Anuradha Mathur and Dilip da Cunha, *Soak: Mumbai in an Estuary* (New Delhi: Rupa & Co., 2009).

12 Both authors chose to use embroidery as a method of investigation; the process and experience of embroidery is specific to Akshar.

Akshar Gajjar,
Bhavya Jain

13 Debjani Bhattacharyya, *Empire and Ecology in the Bengal Delta: The Making of Calcutta*, Studies in Environment and History (Cambridge: Cambridge University Press, 2018).

14 We borrow 'soak' as a way of imagining land-water relationships from Mathur and Da Cunha, *Soak* (see note 11).

15 Paola Viganò, "The Territory as a Subject 1," in *Designing Landscape Architectural Education* (Abingdon, Oxon; New York, NY: Routledge, Taylor Group, 2021), 325–33.

Debjani Bhattacharyya's work on the Bengal Delta and its urban land- and waterscapes shows how folk representations like songs, paintings and embroidery warn us about the ethical limits of fixing nature's mobility through a regime of ownership and separation.[13] Stitching the lines of flowing water allows for thinking about its fluid movement through the landscape. The water bank is not a line but a gradient. The time taken to embroider the flows of water creates a realization of its unbound nature: it flows in and out of said bank, depositing silt and thus also shifting the land around. Much work on mapping in the 1800s discusses the colonial project of creating binaries of land and water – human and non-human – for ease of governance. When shown through threads and knots, the overflowing water and the subsequent sedimentation blurs boundaries between land and water. Multiple bodies of water meet land in nebulous interrelations: be it land soaked in water, or water interspersed with floating land, one cannot say.[14] On a Cartesian map, territory becomes an object to be observed; this vision freezes landscape processes in time and space rather than understanding them as continuously evolving. In the flat top view of the trigonometric survey maps as well as contemporary GIS mappings of river systems, the temporal processes of landscape formations are lost. Water systems are far from being frozen in time; not only is the water continuously moving, but it is also transporting elements from microscopic sediments to larger rocks, thereby shaping and reshaping its banks. Contrary to this abstract understanding, embroidery encourages engagement with the water, with sediments, plants, mud and the like as subjects.[15] As soon as water is read as a subject, it becomes evident that its current state of being is not a given but rather a product of different processes occurring in long and short temporalities. As water approaches a mound of land in the middle of the river, it slows down. This deceleration makes space for plant growth, which invites fish, birds and insects to feed and live. Embroidering this work created the opportunity to inhabit the landscape while representing it. We conjecture that a similar experience would have guided the process of making the Kashmiri map shawls, adding to their rich and multilayered human, non-human narratives.

The tactility of embroidery allows for an intricate reading of the landscape. It offers an opportunity to unpack and respond to the relationships of land, water, flora and fauna. Embroidery involves holding the landscape while stitching; this marks a fundamental shift in our way of experiencing the water-land relationship. Colonial cartographies such as (**FIG. B**), by contrast, show this landscape from the top alone. Embroidery, however, forces a focus on particular parts – land, water, bank, vegetation – while representing it, allowing closeness and intimacy. The temporal aspect of embroidering opens up another perspective on the landscape: embroidering is a slow, continuous process, often involving repetitive stitches; this slow reading of territory allows more time to acknowledge its continuous shifts and changes. In the face of multiple water-related crises – floods, drought, health and liveability – embroidery offers profound departures from the dominant tools of mapping that are still underpinned by their colonial predecessors. •

C

LEFT
Embroidered tapestry engaging the various elements of land and waterscapes by Akshar Gajjar. Image by authors.

Liquid Shadows

Valentina Noce ventures into the eerie realm of water, drawing parallels to Pascal's abyss. Through 'Liquid Shadows,' she creates a digital odyssey, exploring water's unsettling essence, mysterious allure and haunting ambiguity.

Valentina Noce

The anecdote of 'Pascal's abyss' traces a discourse around the construction of fear and anxiety in a critical space. Allegedly, after an accident in 1654, French mathematician, inventor and philosopher Blaise Pascal (1623–1662) was haunted by a horrific void at his side. From this obsession, reflection on the void evolved into a theoretical examination of the ambiguity of blank space and shadow. Amplifying the compendium on the discourse on void and fear, *water* – as a spatial stage of unease – assimilates and recalls the grammar of Pascal's abyss. The narrative of the unsettling and uncanny qualities of water unfolds spaces made up of flowing ghosts, foggy mermaids, wet *doppelgängers*. Observing a reflection in the water that fails to mirror its source, the project 'Liquid Shadows' reports the unforeseen, moving void within it. Running a digital homeopathic operation, the images accumulate into a visual realm created through repetition, scanning, layering, stretching and edulcorating – portraying water as an unsettling and unhomely space. These visuals suggest the inherent ambiguity of water. Closely observing water generates an archive of uncertain, disguised, liquid shadows. •

1 Anthony Vidler, *Warped Space* (Cambridge, MA: MIT Press, 2002).

ALL IMAGES
Collage. Sabotage Practice / Valentina Noce, 2024.

Liquid Shadows

Valentina Noce

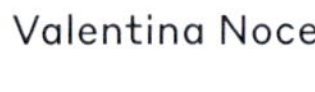

Valentina Noce

Not a Drop Is Lost

Following a week-long student excursion to Banyalbufar in Mallorca (Spain) organized by Professor Teresa Galí-Izard, Stefan Breit and Insa Jelena Streit from the Chair of Being Alive at ETH Zürich contemplated the irrigation system and documented their encounters with a geologist, a historian, two caretakers of the water infrastructure and a tomato gardener.

Stefan Breit,
Insa Jelena Streit

Our trip to Banyalbufar, Spain, takes place at the end of October 2023. The public bus from Palma takes us on a narrow, winding road over the Serra de Tramuntana, the mountain range that stretches along the northwest coast of the Balearic island of Mallorca. After numerous turns, the bus winds down in serpentines and the village becomes visible before us.
The scenery is incredible:

> Clinging to the slope, Banyalbufar appears like a majestic staircase of cultivated terraces descending to the sea and opening towards it.[1]

Banyalbufar is located directly above the Balearic Sea, with the steep slopes of the mountain Mola de Planícia in the background. From the mountain forest to the sea cliffs, stone-walled terraces run through the entire village (FIG. B). The summer season is almost over; it is the last week that the hotels are still open before the winter break. As usual, it has been a hot and dry summer. Mallorca has a typical Mediterranean summer climate, which is characterized by a long and severe drought from mid-April to September and a peak of rainfall in autumn. To deal with these conditions, the people of Banyalbufar have developed their own approach to managing water and have turned the scarce resource into a precious commodity. Bartomeu Barceló Pons, Jean-Pierre Deffontaines and Onofre Rullán Salamanca describe the centrality of water for Banyalbufar:

> Water is the wealth of Banyalbufar. It is the element that turns the municipality into a true hanging garden. But the wealth is due to ingenious domestication of water. During spring, not a drop of water reaches the sea.[2]

We are here to be inspired by this special relationship with water. Through this essay, we seek to reflect on what we have learned in order to document and share it with others. In doing so, we join the travellers who have visited and published about Banyalbufar before us.[3] The local population never felt the need to document the terraced landscape and the water system in writing. An old woman from the village tells us:

1 Ambrois Régis, Pierre Frapa and Sébastien Giorgis, *Paysages de terrasses* (Aix-en-Provence: Edisund, 1993), 108.

2 Bartomeu Barceló Pons, Jean-Pierre Deffontaines and Onofre Rullán Salamanca, *Banyalbufar, geografia i medi ambient* (Banyalbufar: Associació Cultural Bany-Al-Bahar, 2009).

3 See references made in this essay.

A

CURRENT PAGE
A water reservoir surrounded by gardens and agricultural fields. Photo: Chair of Being Alive, 2023.

> If someone came from outside and bought land in the community, they didn't understand the logic and the rules behind the system. Local people used it so naturally that they have never thought to write it down.[4]

Until recently, the preservation of the water infrastructure survived through oral knowledge, nurtured by endless hours of work on the terraces, passed down from one generation to the next. But now that is slowly changing, and with change comes the need for documentation. We are fully aware that we cannot fill this gap. Nevertheless, we are convinced that the Banyalbufar model serves as a great source of inspiration, not only for places that are or will be plagued by drought, but for all landscape projects that seek to harmonize interventions with local natural conditions rather than working against them. Banyalbufar has resisted more extractive forms of water management, continuing with traditional modes of cultivation that reflect a deep understanding of the limitation of resources and long-term production.

In the following sections of this essay, we weave our findings into descriptions of our encounters with local experts and practitioners during the excursion. In doing so, we provide a multi-perspectival portrayal of the water infrastructure as it currently stands.[5]

ENCOUNTER WITH A GEOLOGIST

On our first morning we meet with a geologist who drove here from Palma. He takes us on a tour around the village. We begin our journey at the base of the cliffs and make our way up to the main road, where we have a panoramic view of the landscape. Along our hike, he carries a large drawing pad, which he uses to sketch while explaining to us: "To understand the availability of freshwater is to understand the relationship between precipitation and geology." Precipitation seeps away into the ground and accumulates underground above impermeable geologic layers. In the Serra de Tramuntana, the geologic strata rise towards the Balearic Sea. Therefore, most freshwater moves in the opposite direction, towards the heartland of the island. The main aquifers gather on the southern side of the mountain ridge. Banyalbufar receives its water from a number of small fountains located at an altitude of 200 to 400 metres just above the village. The fountains' flow rates are irregular – varying not only between seasons, but also between rainy and arid years; overall, they are not particularly high. Fountains run on the northern side of the Mola de Planícia because of a minor overflow of water from the local aquifer located below the southern slope of the mountain, facing the neighbouring village, Esporles. This hydrogeological condition has created natural water scarcity in Banyalbufar. The geologist remarks: "In a drought, Banyalbufar will be the first town without water."

It is this specific local condition of water scarcity that has made close management of the resource a necessity. The inhabitants simply had to adapt. The geologist also points out that the mountainsides facing the Balearic Sea are prone to erosion due to salt-heavy winds and tectonic pressure. Therefore, a thick bed of eroded rocks has accumulated on the hillside of the Mola de Planícia. The pile of debris alters the section of the slope, forming a plateau underneath the mountain peak. The plateau ends with a steep slope descending towards the coast. This is where the village of Banyalbufar is located and where the inhabitants have terraced the terrain:

> The boulders literally lie on the ground. Inhabitants could just grab the stones from the ground and build walls and houses without needing to cut or split the rock.

The geologist concludes that these geological conditions – debris beds being formed along the coastline of the Serra de Tramuntana – have been fundamental to the formation of the terraced landscape.

ENCOUNTER WITH A HISTORIAN

At sunset, we gather in the courtyard of our hotel, surrounded by very old walls and floors built with stones that once belonged to the estate of the Baron of Banyalbufar. We meet a local historian who begins his remarks on Banyalbufar with an etymology of the name:

> The name *Banyalbufar* was given by Moorish inhabitants who founded the settlement in the tenth century. The original name, *Bany-al-bahar*, comprises two different components, both of Arabic origin: *banya* [constructed] and *bahar* [by the sea]. The original meaning of Banyalbufar is, therefore, 'founded by the sea.'

After their arrival, the Moors began building stone walls to cultivate the steep slopes, just as they had done in their homelands in North Africa. Over the centuries, over 200 kilometres of dry stone walls were built from local stones by masons called *maestros* [stone masters].[6] Various vegetables and cereals were initially grown on the terraces for the residents' own consumption. From the fourteenth century onwards, grapes became the most important crop. Table grapes, raisins, vinegar and, of course, wine were increasingly produced. Banyalbufar was, and still is, particularly famous for its Malvasía wine – a typical variety from the Middle Ages known for its high alcohol content, heaviness and sweetness. After a few centuries of production, however, the cultivation of grapes suddenly came to a halt:

> Grapes were practically grown as a monoculture, very close together on the narrow terraces. This did not go well. It was in the nineteenth century, as the small but devastating grape phylloxera [*Phylloxera vastatrix*] appeared. The insect feeds on the roots and leaves of grapevines, gradually cutting off the flow of nutrients and water to the upper parts of the plant. It killed entire vineyards, thousands of plants on the slopes of the village, and people had to uproot and cut down the vines. After the disease, only two individual plants survived without damage.

After this disaster, a new lucrative crop had to be found to satisfy the village's economic needs. The tomato plant, which had already been growing scattered on the terraces, was selected for large-scale cultivation in the nineteenth century.[7] However, unlike its deep-rooted predecessors, which required minimal watering in the first two to three years, the nightshade tomato has high water demands. This led to the modification of some of the existing terraces, which were retrofitted with an irrigation system.

A tree-like network of water channels was constructed, connecting an underground aquifer above the village with the terraces all the way to the sea. Along this network of channels, cemented reservoirs, known as *tanques* or *jafarechs*,[8] were added using the existing dry stone walls as a base structure (**FIG. H, C**). Each reservoir has a simple watergate that can redirect the flow of water from the channel into the reservoir. The historian emphasizes the different historical origins of these two important structures on the slopes:

> It is absolutely essential to understand that the terraces and the water infrastructure are historically two different things. The terraces date back to the origin of the village in the tenth century, while the channels and reservoirs were added much later, in the twentieth century.

4 All quotes from inhabitants and local experts are anonymized.

5 See note 4.

6 Régis et al., *Paysages de terrasses* (see note 1), 108.

7 Pons et al., *Banyalbufar, geografia i medi ambient* (see note 2), 83.

8 Régis et al., *Paysages de terrasses* (see note 1), 108.

B C

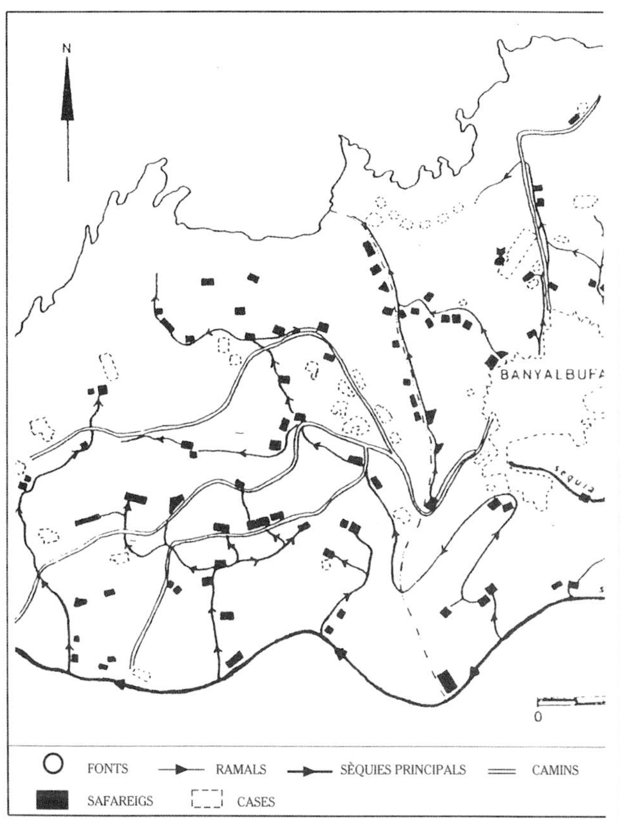

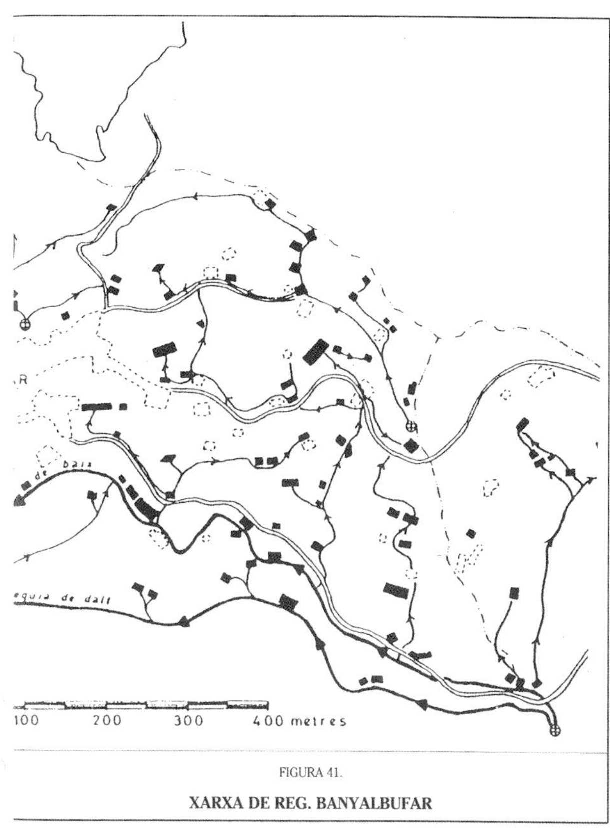

B Terraced landscape of Banyalbufar stretching from the mountains to the sea. Photo: Chair of Being Alive, 2023.

C Map showing the flow of water from the source to the sea through a network of channels and reservoirs. Maria Antònia Carbonero Gamundí, *L'espai de l'Aigua*, (Palma de Mallorca: Consell Insular de Mallorca, 1992), 238–39.

Above all, the water infrastructure is an ingenious invention. It deals with the scarcity of water created by the specific climate and geology of Banyalbufar in an intelligent and careful way. By filling the reservoirs in winter, when the spring is running, enough water is available to irrigate the plants in summer. The system of canals and reservoirs retains all the available water and holds it in reserve for irrigation. Not a drop of water is lost on its way to the sea. Over 150 cemented reservoirs of varying sizes – but often measuring ten metres wide, twenty metres long and five metres deep – can store up to 1 000 m³ of water, for a total of 150 000 m³ of water that is temporarily stored along the slope above the village.[9]

Today, international tourism transformed the original agrarian society of Mallorca into a service economy. Richard Branson, one of the richest men on earth, has just opened a five-star hotel in the neighbouring village. There is a golf course and fine restaurants.

Nowadays, almost half of the terraces in Banyalbufar lack the manual labour needed for maintenance and cultivation. As such, they are taken over by pioneer species that nobody planted. On the parts still under cultivation, we find pomegranate, lemon, olive, fig and almond trees, tomato plants, grapevines and grazing ponies (**FIG. A**). Many reservoirs that were once filled with water are now empty and left to deteriorate.

ENCOUNTER WITH CARETAKERS OF THE IRRIGATION SYSTEM

We meet with two caretakers of the irrigation system in front of our hotel. Both men are in their eighties and have lived their whole lives in Banyalbufar. They are part of the *comunitat de regants* [community of irrigators], a local association that aims to maintain the irrigation system. They take us up a steep road towards the Font de la Vila [fountain of the village], near the main channel. One of them points out that there is a strict line between the irrigated and unirrigated sections: "Below the main channel are the irrigated fields; above, the forest. The main channel is the dividing line."

From there, gravity takes the spring water downwards through a network of channels. The channels are small (with a diameter comparable to that of a rain gutter) and were built by hand. Sometimes, they run on the rims of reservoirs (**FIG. G**); sometimes, next to the street. The original sluices are open-air. The watergate covering the inlet of the reservoir is a rectangular ceramic tile that irrigators can remove (**FIG. E**). Over time, many channels, especially the ones at street level, have been covered with concrete slabs. Some channels have been retrofitted with plastic pipes that are placed in the original bed (**FIG. F**). One of our guides opens a drain cover and reveals a sluice – a knot where three different plastic pipes come together. This is the point in the system where the water is distributed among the users.

In Banyalbufar, the allocation of water is regulated according to one's right to water. These rights are attached to properties. A property is measured by the number of tomato plants that can be sustained and irrigated. But over time, the water rights of many properties became disproportional to the size of the land. At a certain point, people started to trade their water rights independently. The municipality reacted and forbade these trades. Now, when a property is sold in parts, the water rights attached to the property have to be split according to the same ratio.

The 'right to water' originates from an ancient water monopoly that applied to about half of the properties in Banyalbufar. Even today, some properties have no water rights at all, and inhabitants have to irrigate from accumulated rain or other sources. The caretakers tell us that, paradoxically, it is the people who have the least water privileges that have built themselves the biggest reservoirs:

9 Régis et al., *Paysages de terrasses* (see note 1), 108.

> Imagine that you have a piece of land. You need a lot of water to irrigate your plants but your water privilege is low. You will only use the water in summer to irrigate. So you have October, November, December, January, February to accumulate water. You have your fixed water rights and you put that in your reservoir until it is filled. Somehow you really don't want to lose the right to water that you have.

Because the fountains' flow rates are irregular, and a fixed amount of water is impossible to guarantee, each user's right to water is translated into a time slot. The rhythm of life is significantly influenced by the rhythm of water distribution:

> The distribution of water is 24 hours per day. It's day and night. Maybe you have your water between 3 a.m. and 4 a.m. in the morning. Tuesday every other week from 3 a.m. to 4 a.m. It's a moment when you have to go open and close the sluice.

But even the time slots change over the year because they are not defined by the hour but by the position of the sun. Each owner of water rights has an allocated time:

> This moment can change over the year. For example, imagine you have the water seven hours after sunset. But the sunset changes over the year. When it's sunset you go and you stop the water from getting to your neighbour and you get the water for yourself.

Users must get water from the reservoir that precedes them in line. First, they close off the channel next to their reservoir; then, they redirect the water of the previous reservoir back into the main channel. This act of 'going and getting' the water involves walking to the previous reservoir and clearing the channel. The Mallorquín term for this action is *gírar l'aigua*: to turn, rotate, change the orientation of the flow of water.

Each user of the system takes responsibility for the stretch of channel between their own and the previous reservoir, cleans it from debris and repairs it if broken. If a reservoir is abandoned, the area of responsibility automatically increases up to the next active reservoir. This rule makes the system quite flexible and, therefore, resilient. Users only need to keep in touch with their direct neighbours to negotiate responsibilities or make changes to the infrastructure. There is no need to understand the system in its entirety. In response to our question regarding whether reservoirs ever spill over, one of our guides explains:

> When it rains a lot, it can happen. Then, the surplus water goes to the torrents. It's always a difficult balance between how much water you can get and how much water you need – because you can also change the type of crop that you cultivate. If you have a lot of water you can have more tomatoes; if you don't have water then that year we only irrigate every other row of tomatoes. It's like playing in extreme conditions.

ENCOUNTER WITH A TOMATO GARDENER

In front of her house, just off the main road, we meet a gardener who has spent her whole life cultivating the terraces of Banyalbufar. In addition to olive oil, she and her family have mainly grown tomatoes and continue to do so on a smaller scale. These are the tomatoes that the historian has already told us about. Introduced in the nineteenth century, they have become widely recognized not only throughout the island, but also across the Spanish mainland.

> We grow a tomato called *ramellet*. The most typical dish you must eat in Banyalbufar is *pan con tomate*. You cut a tomato in half and rub it on a freshly toasted slice of bread. The flesh of the tomato remains on the bread, the skin can be thrown away. Then you add olive oil and salt. It's so simple, but so delicious.

Before we visit the tomato plants in her fields, the gardener shows us the attic of her house, which serves as a storage room for the tomatoes. Countless small nails on the roof beams are used to hang them in bundles to dry (**FIG. D**).

> The special thing about our tomatoes is that we preserve them whole. From midsummer to the beginning of winter, we harvest the ripe tomatoes in the morning hours, because then the water content of the tomatoes is higher. Equipped with a thread and a needle, we assemble them one by one to form a rosary, called *rosario* or *ramellet*. These rosaries, weighing around four kilos, are hung to dry under the roofs of the village houses. As the skin of the tomatoes is so thick, only the outer layer dries and the inside remains fresh. This means that we can still enjoy the tomatoes almost just as fresh a year after the harvest.

The widespread cultivation of the tomato plant changed the architecture of the village. When the ramellet was introduced, people simply built a wooden attic on top of the small houses to create space for storing and drying the fruit – the tomato made the village grow one storey higher. We leave the attic and go behind the house. There we see the tomato plants, which have already withered but are still bearing fruit. They are supported by a structure made of pine branches.

> Planting tomatoes needs a lot of planning. It is essential to prepare the soil before planting the tomatoes. You could fertilize the soil with animal poop or with chemicals. But I never use chemicals. I use the manure from my chickens and sheep.

If you look closely between the tomato plants, you discover a water reservoir hidden in the stone wall and covered by the terrace above. From there, the tomato gardener can redirect the water to the fields to irrigate the thirsty plants. "I use the water system because I don't want it to get lost."

The tomatoes are no longer available for purchase in the village, because they are only grown for self-consumption. But the harvest was good this year, and the tomato gardener wants us to try the typical dish. She gives us a tomato rosary for our very first pan con tomate later by the sea.

AN ISLAND WITHIN AN ISLAND

Banyalbufar is an island within an island. Its irrigation system can serve as an antithesis to Mallorca's extractive water management, which has long outsized the landscapes' hydrological limits. In addition to the natural water deposits, rainwater is collected in two reservoir lakes in the Serra de Tramuntana and freshwater is generated in energy-extensive desalination plants along the coast. In certain regions, freshwater has to be delivered by water trucks. It seems that one potential answer to the contemporary challenge of Mallorca's water scarcity can be found on the island itself.

In Banyalbufar, there is reciprocity between the landscape and its inhabitants. Local geologic conditions created an abundance of available boulders, which the inhabitants skilfully turned into dry-wall construction. The imbalance of arid summers and heavy rainfall in autumn led the inhabitants to build an infrastructure for water retention and to form a close community to

negotiate care for the system. The continuous flow of water disciplines the inhabitants to match their rhythm of life to the rhythm of the water. The tomato plant demanded room for storage and drying and inspired a new typology of attics.

This approach to living in a close reciprocal relationship with the landscape allowed the inhabitants to realize its inherent potential. By recognizing the constraints of the climate and using the resources available, they turned the landscape into a productive garden. Today, however, the irrigation system is kept alive by the retirees of the village. The younger generation cannot make the same commitment, as many of them work in Palma and only come home at weekends. On the one hand, there is the risk that, with the people, the practices, knowledge and experience will also eventually be lost. On the other, there is the latent potential of the material infrastructure: the dry walls, channels, sluice systems and reservoirs. Most elements are still intact. When not in use, however, they eventually deteriorate. Therefore, many abandoned reservoirs are filled with a small amount of water, just enough to cover the bottom to prevent plants from growing and breaking up the concrete. While the future of the system remains uncertain, the reservoirs lie dormant, bearing the potential of being reactivated. •

D

Drying tomatoes in the attic of a tomato gardener. Photo: Chair of Being Alive, 2023.

Stefan Breit,
Insa Jelena Streit

E F G H

E Ceramic watergate. Photo: Chair of Being Alive, 2023.

F Retrofitting of the irrigation channels with plastic tubes. Photo: Chair of Being Alive, 2023.

G Water flowing into a reservoir. Photo: Chair of Being Alive, 2023.

H A water reservoir built next to an existing dry stone wall. Photo: Chair of Being Alive, 2023.

On Thirst: Anecdotes on Chasing Hidden Waters

Elanz Najar Najafi and Negar Sanaan Bensi delve into the historical and cultural perceptions of thirst and its impact on settlements and cultivation within the deserts of the Iranian Plateau. By challenging the negative connotations associated with thirst and exploring the innovative water management techniques of inhabitants, they reveal how thirst has been a positive driving force for imagination, care and the nurturing of life in arid environments.

Elanz Najar Najafi,
Negar Sanaan Bensi

In the view of the French colonizers, the Saharan desert was "a land of thirst and fear, from which all life was reputedly absent."[1] Thirst was understood as a negative polydipsic condition with quantitative features, associated with an absence of life and with fear, that determined survival in the barren environment of the desert. This essay questions the negative connotations of 'thirst' by drawing on the act of chasing hidden waters in the *biābān* [Persian for desert]. Presented through a selection of anecdotes, reflections on poems, historical reports, engravings and photographs, this chase reveals the spatialization and materialization of 'thirst' in the landscape and territories of the Iranian Plateau.

Geographically, much of the Middle East lies within the arid belt, characterized by low precipitation and limited accessible bodies of water such as lakes and rivers. As a result, the region – and its life – largely depends on underground aquifers. Most prosperous cities in the Iranian Plateau have been built in deserts near underground water reservoirs. Here, inhabitants cultivated the land through specific techniques of chasing hidden waters,[2] grafting and water-sharing systems. Despite limitations, they created gardens and expanded cities upon and towards gardens. They even built ice-storage facilities to enjoy cool water and syrups in the summer. How were all these remarkable achievements possible?

Arguably, the inhabitants of this territory did not perceive and treat issues around water quantifiably as 'lacks' and 'emptiness.' In other words, their effort to inhabit the desert was not focused on exploiting large amounts of water. Instead, what made life in the desert possible was 'becoming thirsty' and chasing the water – in other words, reaching the very essence of life, through thirst.

In Avestan, *taršna* [thirst] is an etymological transformation of *ters* [dry, to dry] and *terra* [earth, dry land]; it indicates the 'territory' in the urge to actualize the invisibilities of a desert, directly relating it to the very idea of the biābān as being somewhere that requires 'care' and 'nourishment' for it to be inhabited [*Ābād*].[3] While thirst may evoke discomfort, it in fact guarantees our survival: if we did not become thirsty, we would not endure. Often, one is better able to perceive water's taste and freshness after long being thirsty. In the desert, where the most important sources of water are hidden from view, the notion of 'thirst' becomes a historical and collective state rather than a short-term personal sensation. In such an environment, thirst indicates that water – a valuable and vital entity – should not be used except to create something more valuable and vital than water itself.

Water in the desert is invisible; it is a 'latent potentiality' that requires mediation to become actual and accessible. It is thirst that mediates this process by motivating *khayāl* [imagination]. *Alam al-khayāl* is an intermediate world with its own space, passage of time, colours and forms, where events occur in a real, but not necessarily actual, manner. It is an isthmus that Persian Muslim philosophers called the *mundus imaginalis* [imaginal world] – not the creation of humankind's whims and fancies but a world that possesses an ontological reality of its own.[4] This isthmian bordering space "is the medium through which the delivery of world from potentiality to act is effected."[5]

In his poems, the fourteenth-century Iranian poet Hafez grandly and gracefully praises the stream of Ruknābād, so much so that centuries later, British journalist and politician Lord Curzon (1859–1925), travelling in Shiraz, chose to visit this stream. Curzon was bitterly surprised when he saw Ruknābād's "slender" water, writing:

> It is after crossing the subsequent ridge of the Kūh-e-Bamū that we notice, by the roadside, a tiny channel filled with running water that accompanies us for some distance on our march. Lest none should guess it, let me say that this slender rivulet is no less a stream than the Ruknābād, which, rising in the hills twelve miles away, races gaily down to Shiraz, and is celebrated by the patriotic Hafiz in terms that would lead one to expect some less insignificant channel.[6]

Curzon's misunderstanding of Hafez's descriptions of Ruknābād reveals something important: for Hafez, the khayāl of Ruknābād is greater than its actual size. If a large river had flowed through Shiraz, Hafez would probably not have written a poem to glorify it. But the British Curzon is alien to the grandeur of the khayāl of precious water, having come to Iran from a lush landscape with vast rivers. In the same way, the khayāl of water is greater than its quantity for someone who is thirsty. Throughout Persian literature, thirst is praised in a similar way. One verse that has become an allegory in everyday language invites people to be thirsty instead of looking for a large amount of water.[7] It considers thirst to be the key to chasing water. Similar verses describe not only the thirsty pursuer in search of water but also the water in search of a true thirsty seeker.[8]

In the desert, the scant water that reaches the ground during short rainfalls has three possible destinies: it flows on the surface as floods and streams; it wets the shallow depth of the soil, mostly evaporating when the sun heats the ground; or it penetrates to the depth of the ground and reaches underground aquifers. Thirst motivates inhabitants of deserts to seek the smallest signs, presences and absences in the landscape, air and sky, to carefully measure every drop of this water in any form or state and to employ complex techniques to extract these waters. Of these, one of the most widespread is the *qanāt*, a subterranean system that allows hidden water to gradually emerge over the ground.[9]

ON 'THIRST' AND MEASURING EACH DROP OF WATER

One morning King Nāser al-Dīn Shāh Qājār[10] woke up and saw a good rain coming. It was one of the last days of summer and

1 Samia Henni, ed., *Deserts Are Not Empty* (New York, NY: Columbia Books on Architecture and the City, 2022), 1.

2 Abū Bakr ibn Muhammad ibn al Husayn Al-Karajī, *Kitāb Inbāt al-miyāh al-khafīyah* (1674), Rare Book & Manuscript Library, University of Pennsylvania, Lawrence J. Schoenberg Collection, LJS 399.

3 *Ābād* is a Persian term (*āpāt* in Middle Persian and ā-*pāta* in Old Persian) derived from the Indo-European word *Pā*(*y*), meaning to take care, protect and educate. Mohammad Hassandoust, *An Etymological Dictionary of Persian Language* (Tehran: Academy of Persian Language and Literature, 2016), 3–4.

4 Seyyed Hossein Nasr, "The World of the Imagination and the Concept of Space in Persian Miniatures," *Islamic Quarterly* 13, no. 3 (July 1969): 131.

5 Patrick Healy, *The Model and its Architecture* (Rotterdam: 010 Publishers, 2008), 165.

6 George Nathaniel Curzon (1st Marquess Curzon of Kedleston), *Persia and the Persian Question,* vol. 2 (London: Longmans, Green, and Co., 1892), 93.

7 آب کم جو تشنگی آور به دست / تا بجوشد آبت از بالا و پست, Jalāl al-Dīn Muḥammad Rūmī (1207–1273).

On Thirst: Anecdotes on Chasing Hidden Waters

Elanz Najar Najafi,
Negar Sanaan Bensi

he rejoiced, saying: "each drop of this rain is worth an *ashrafi*[11] [a gold coin]."[12] This statement carries more than mere emotion. In the Iranian Plateau, water was measured and distributed according to the scale of a *fenjān* [cup],[13] akin to goldsmiths who measure their precious metals with units of weight like *mithqāl* [4.2 grams] and ounces. It was through these small gauges that water droplets were measured, valued, divided and distributed in the cities, villages, houses and farms. The qanāt itself is in fact the result of gathering droplets of water. The drops that seep and trickle from its shafts gather to form a stream of water that eventually flows into horizontal tunnels towards a city or farm.

ON 'THIRST' AND SEEKING DEEP HIDDEN WATERS

In the *Manṭiq-uṭ-Ṭayr* [The Conference of the Birds],[14] among all the birds present it is the hoopoe that becomes the guide to reach the *simurgh* – a mystical bird representing the ultimate spiritual unity. According to an ancient belief, the hoopoe recognizes the signs of hidden waters in the desert, even when it flies high in the sky. The hoopoe can locate underground water tables and determine their depth, type and volume.

Like the hoopoe discerning the location of water sources with uncanny precision, the main challenge in constructing a qanāt was not that of excavating numerous deep wells or digging lengthy underground tunnels to connect them, but rather that of attaining the same level of certainty regarding the presence of a substantial and delicious underground water table at an appropriate depth. This highlights the daunting task of detecting the most inconspicuous element of life: a colourless, odourless and formless substance.

Thirst induced the inhabitants of the desert to recognize the presence of deep water through the type of stones, the colour of the soil, the growth of certain types of plants and the presence of some of the smallest animals and insects. There was little room for trial and error: the initial well had to yield the desired result and provide sufficient water. For that reason, an important and honourable profession emerged: that of the *moqqader* [one who knows the measures and values], known as the master of finding hidden waters.

However, accessing underground water was not solely achieved by digging a qanāt. In cases where the underground water basin level was insufficient to justify digging a qanāt, alternative methods were employed, such as camelthorn-dependent cultivation.

Camelthorns (genus *Alhagi*) are salt-loving, drought-resistant desert plants that depend on reaching deep, invisible waters for survival. A thousand years ago, in his unique treatise entitled *Inbāt al-miyāh al-khafīyah* [The Extraction of Hidden Waters], Karajī recounts the story of a qanāt-digger who, while digging a tunnel, saw the root of a camelthorn growing more than fifty cubits (twenty-five meters) into the ground to reach the water. Building on this, Karajī explains how, in some regions, the optimal yield of melons and watermelons is achieved by embedding their seeds inside the stem of a camelthorn, and there are numerous other plants that can be cultivated in a similar way. This reference is a prelude to an extraordinary method of farming that relies upon chasing water deep within the desert landscape.

Two centuries later, Rashid al-Din Hamadāni provided a more detailed explanation of this method: in some areas, a small slit is made at the taproot of the camelthorn and a germinated, soaked watermelon or melon seed is placed within this slit and covered with soil. Due to its permanent access to moisture, the thorn's root continuously delivers water to the seed, nurturing what results in an exceptionally sweet fruit.[15] This technique represents a grafting method whereby the root becomes the holder of another seed: it cares for and carries the

8 تشنگان گر آب جویند از جهان / آب هم جوید به عالم تشنگان , Ibid.

9 The *qanāt* comprises vertical shafts of successively increasing depth connected by a *dehliz* [horizontal underground tunnel], which directs the water from subterranean sources down a slight incline to gardens, farms and settlements.

10 Naser al-Din Shah was the fourth king of the Qajar Dynasty in Iran. He reigned from 1848 until 1896, when he was assassinated.

11 The *ashrafi* is a gold coin that originated in Mamluk Egypt and was later widely adopted in regions under Muslim rule in the Middle East, Central Asia and South Asia (Wikipedia).

12 Nāser al-Dīn Shāh, Rūznāmeh-ye Khāterāt-e Nāser al-Dīn Shāh Qājār, *Diary of Naser-al-Din Shah of October 1890 to September 1891*, ed. Majid Abde Amin and Nasrin Khalili (Tehran: Research Institute for Cultural Heritage and Tourism, 2015), 44.

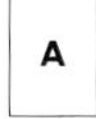

LEFT
Tabas deserts, Iran, view towards a *qanāt* with palms planted in the furnaces of the vertical shafts, photograph by authors.

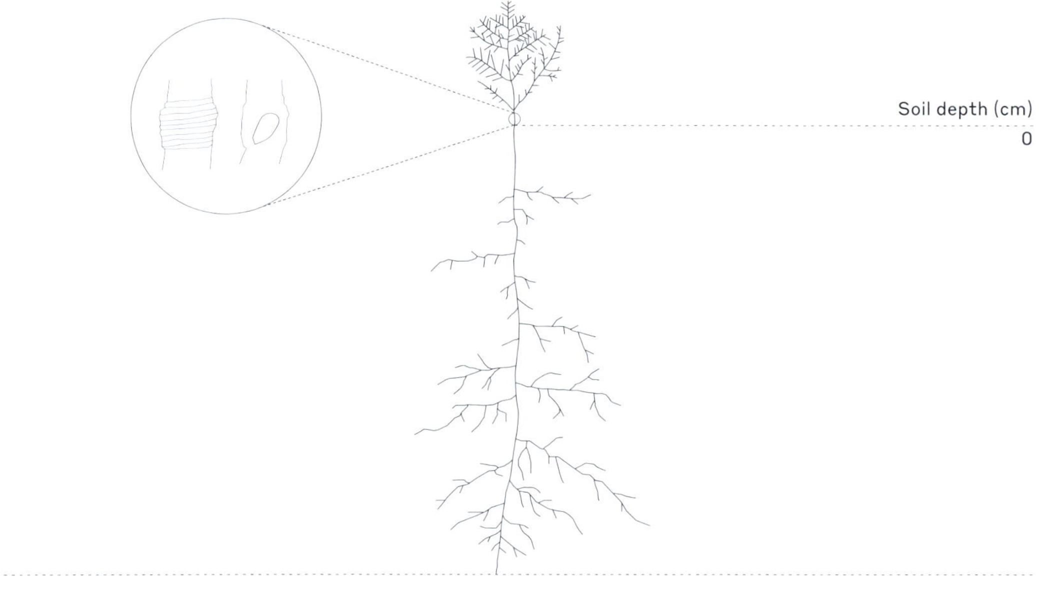

Elanz Najar Najafi,
Negar Sanaan Bensi

13 *Fenjān* is a traditional measuring scale that turns a unit of volume unit into a unit of time, and time into a surface unit. It was a medium through which the land and its productivity were measured based on a qanāt's water capacity and its distribution on land.

14 *The Conference of the Birds*, or Speech of the Birds (منطق الطیر) is Sheikh Farid ad-Din Attār Nishāburī's (1145–1221) most famous work and one of the unique masterpieces of Persian mystical literature.

15 Rashid al-Din Fadl Allah al-Hamadāni, *Āsār wa Ahyā*, ed. Iraj Afshar and Manuchehr Sotudeh (Tehran: McGill University Press, 1989), 177.

16 Michael Marder, "Grafting," in *Graft*, ed. idem (Minneapolis: University of Minnesota Press, 2016), 15.

17 Sīrjān is a city in Kermān province, southern Iran.

B

C

B Grafting a melon seed in a camelthorn's taproot.

C Grafting melon in camelthorns, Zali village, Esfarāyen, Iran. Photograph by Ahmad Nikgoftar.

'latent potentiality' of giving life to another being. The grafters could thus imagine and recognize in the camelthorn, which is hostile and dry like the desert itself, the possibility of life in the "constitutive capacity for symbiosis."[16]

Sīrjāni[17] farmers recognized that the camelthorn's roots pull water up from the depths of the ground like a lamp wick and store it in their stem. Following a longstanding belief, they avoided burning camelthorns, which can be the best fuel for ovens and stoves in the treeless landscape of the deserts. They also believed that all thorns would burn in hell – with the exception of the camelthorn.[18] This prodigious vegetable farming technique has persisted until recently in different areas in Iran, including Kermān, Semnān, Fārs, Khorāsān, Isfahān and Shūshtar.

ON 'THIRST' AND SEEKING TRAPPED MOISTURE

In the easternmost borders of Kāshān lies a place known as Band-e-Rig, characterized by its undulating sand fields. The wind's force has created ridges, hills, large mounds and wide pits.[19] With the slightest rain in the winter, these barren lands become flooded, muddy and impassable; in the summer, as the wind blows, sand and dust arise, disturbing the nearby settlements. Despite such hardships, the inhabitants of these deserts have discovered the presence of trapped moisture underneath the topsoil of the dry and wavy sand.

In this barren area, where the annual rainfall rarely exceeds eighty millimetres, it is enough to remove seventy centimetres of the surface sand to feel the soil's moisture. "At the beginning of the spring, the farmers carve the sand with a spade,"[20] and in each hole, they plant several soaked watermelon seeds with a little fertilizer and leave them for a while.[21] The seeds grow with the presence of moisture and their roots reach the water underneath. In the event of rain and hardened ground, farmers count on the collective force of multiple sprouts, which eventually break through the soil and emerge.[22] When six leaves appear, the farmers leave only one plant in each hole and remove the rest; doing so allows the remaining plant to thrive with the moisture of the soil.[23]

Since the sand dunes are extremely fluid, the farmers twist the long vines and curly tendrils of the sprouted watermelons around the stalks of camelthorns, ensuring that they remain stable.[24] "Saline soil is hotter than non-salty soil, which helps melons and watermelons mature more gradually."[25] In the desert, temperature fluctuations are extreme, and the salinity of the soil retains heat, making products sweeter. Despite this scorching sun, fresh and sweet watermelons and melons provide a refreshing remedy. Watermelons grown with no watering effort offer cool and pleasant juice, providing respite from the heat.

ON 'THIRST' AND SEEKING FLOOD STREAMS

The Qazvīn Plain is an alluvial fan located on the southern slopes of the Alborz mountain range. The difference in height between the mountain slopes and the low plains in the Qazvīn region causes seasonal flash floods, often in spring and autumn. At times, it can rain for dozens of days, followed by devastating floods that engulf the whole plain. Over time, inhabitants of the plain came to understand the nature of these waters: they consist of a small volume of water flowing at high speed from steep mountain passes. The destructive power of these floods is not so much related to the quantity of the flowing water but rather to its velocity.

Notwithstanding, for the rest of the year, only limited underground water can be used via qanāts. Such 'thirsty' conditions have compelled inhabitants of this plain not only to search for ways to halt and control the flash floods, but also to harness their potential as a valuable source, as a precious gift; they have

On Thirst: Anecdotes on Chasing Hidden Waters

Elanz Najar Najafi, Negar Sanaan Bensi

creatively constructed productive gardens all around the city of Qazvīn. The gardens of Qazvīn, especially those in the northern flood-prone areas, act as a horizontal damming system. They gradually reduce the speed and destructive force of the water, allowing it to inundate the land and facilitating water absorption into underground aquifers.

The gardens of Qazvīn were built on a dry plain, drawing on water brought by annual floods rather than on water from qanāts. Although irrigated only once a year, the gardens were fruitful and boasted various trees. These gardens lacked fences or walls, so that water could flow unimpeded from one garden to another. As a result, specific social relations and ownership mechanisms based on collective and collaborative decision-making were implemented to ensure the security of these gardens, the city and the whole plain.

CONCLUSION

More than one-fifth of Earth's land area is covered by deserts – the surface of which is increasing as an aftermath of climate change. In this context, reimagining the desert, reconsidering modes of inhabitation and revisiting the techniques of chasing hidden waters is not only necessary but also urgent. Such processes should enable us to envision alternatives to ongoing extractivist and technocratic tendencies that have caused irreversible damage to the fragile ecosystem of the desert landscape over the last two centuries. There is a need to shift from historically dominant colonial perspectives, in which the desert is seen as a place that has been excluded and abandoned, a land of fear, thirst and emptiness. In fact, as this essay has argued, thirst is what motivates khayāl to chase, care for and reveal any trace of hidden waters, moisture and vapor in a desert. Rethinking the desert through the notion of thirst permits access to a world of 'latent potentialities' and mediates their delivery to actuality. In such a reading, thirst is not a negative polydipsic condition approaching death but rather a necessary state of being and becoming in the desert. Thirst shifts the concern of the water seeker from quantity to quality, elevating the grandeur of their imagination. The idiosyncrasy and beauty of cities like Tabas, Kāshān and Yazd did not lie in their access to large amounts of water, but rather in the sophistication of their inhabitants in chasing these hidden waters by amplifying their khayāl. •

18 Morteza Farhadi, "Camelthorn Bush-oriented Cultivation: A Forgotten Cultivation," *Jahad Journal* 134 (October 1990): 22–29 [in Persian].

19 Abdu'l-Rahim Kalantar Zarrabi, *Tārīkh-e Kāshān,* ed. Iraj Afshar (Teheran: Amir Kabir Press, 1999), 106.

20 Zarrabi, *Tārīkh-e Kāshān* (see note 19), 162.

21 Ibid.

22 Ibid.

23 Ibid.

24 Javad Safi-Nejad, *Kāriz dar Iran wa Shīve-haye Sonnati-e BahrebardāriAz* Ān [Qanāt in Iran and the Traditional Ways of Employing It] (Tehran: Pouye Mehr Eshraq, 2016), 718.

25 al-Hamadāni, *Āsār wa Ahyā* (see note 15), 177.

D

LEFT
Chale-sonbak, Band-e-Rig, Kāshān, Iran. Photographs courtesy of @Injairanas.

Men Talk but the Women Fetch the Water

Stavroula Michael examines the coloniality of water infrastructures in Cyprus during late British colonialism and the early years of independence, highlighting how these systems perpetuated systemic inequalities. She unearths hidden histories of water attending neglected narratives of women and their relationships to material constructions such as village fountains.

Stavroula Michael

The *Cyprus Review* was a monthly political newspaper established by the British colonial government in Cyprus in 1942. It continued publishing into the post-war period of welfare development in 1955, at which point it mainly served as propaganda for the colonialists. On April 1, 1949, it reported British Governor Turnbull's visit to the Greek Cypriot village of Patriki. Its headline reads: "This New Scheme Will Aid the WOMEN WHO FETCH THE WATER" [capitals in the original]. Accompanied by a picture of Governor Turnbull turning on a tap, the caption quotes him saying, "What pleases me about your water supply is the way it helps you women-folk."[1] He then defended the Ten-Year Development Plan, addressing the crowd:

> Perhaps none of you has read the Development Plan. Perhaps you have and have thought it has little to do with you. In fact, it means everything to you. It is indeed for you.[2]

Next to the image of Governor Turnbull, a schoolgirl is depicted giving flowers to Mrs Turnbull; both are mute. Another newspaper ironically reported the same event with the title "The Men Talk but the Women Fetch the Water."[3] Addressing these newspaper reports contextually reveals that women and lower-class people were not a primary concern for British colonialists in their visions of development through water infra-structure. This lack of attention to women and the lower class is evident in the symbolism of the visual material produced at the time as well as in the structures and infrastructures of water.

THE COLONIALITY OF DEVELOPMENT, CYPRIOT PEASANT IDENTITY AND WATER INFRASTRUCTURE

The British Governor's performative act took place after the Second World War – a period marked by extensive development projects, the loss of many colonies and the impending like-lihood of losing more, together with the rise of the welfare state in the colonial metropolis. These circumstances led to the rebranding of the Law of Colonial Development as the Law of Colonial Development and *Welfare* [emphasis added]. The Colonial Development and Welfare Act of 1945 was used to fund the Ten-Year Development Plan of 1946 in Cyprus, which prioritized a very particular type of economy – heavily water-dependent agriculture – despite numerous concerns regarding Cyprus's water stress. This attests to both the concept of 'development' and the socio-economic realities of its implementation, which are historically rooted in Western thinking – and specifically colonial European thinking – as discussed by Gustavo Esteva.[4] Esteva has drawn special attention to this significant time in Britain's colonial history, when development was officially linked to 'welfare,' ostensibly for the benefit of its colonial subjects.

Both development and welfare were meant as capital investment that would enable the generation of more profit and the re-establishment of colonialism as a benevolent, modernizing force. In Cyprus, the British oversaw the design and construction of water infrastructure including canals, tanks, reservoirs and borehole drilling to support agriculture as well as to provide water for cities and villages using funds for 'development.' Through the rational recording of water, land and population data, operations were systematized using the means of bureaucracy and policy (maps, legislation etc.). These interventions were all based on certain preconceived British colonial and orientalist notions of Cypriot people as largely 'undeveloped,' on the one hand, and of themselves as truly benevolent on the other – given that the British wished to reinforce their own civilizing European identity by reinstating Greek Cypriot Hellenism.[5]

While these attributes of development were integral to the colonial project, in the case of Cyprus, development had a persistent coloniality – a socio-economic and cultural hegemony that was passed down to the newly established Republic of Cyprus in 1960. The new Five-Year Development Plan prioritized agriculture just as the previous plan had, arguing that it represented "the occupation and nurture of the people."[6] What is also important to note here is that both development plans were drafted for Cyprus by experts in the UK and, after independence, experts in the US. Specifically, most of the points of the Five-Year Development Plan of 1961 were based on a report authored by Willard Thorp on behalf of the United Nations Development Programme.[7] The 1961 report dictated "the effective marshalling of resources and their efficient use" as crucial for development, with water being "the key natural resource." This perpetuated an intensely modernist approach to water infrastructure and further promoted the reliance on agriculture for development, echoing the 'experts' of the 1946 Ten-Year Development Plan. The persistent prioritization of agriculture can also be directly linked to the construction and maintenance of an orientalist portrayal of Cypriots as shepherds, farmers and generally backwards, uncivilized people. The very first High Commissioner of the United Kingdom to Cyprus, Sir Garnet Wolseley (1833–1913), described the capital in 1878 as a "commodious place, clean but in the midst of filthy houses."[8] Such attitudes were reinforced by the photographic expedition of John Thomson (1837–1921) in 1878, described by Greek Cypriot photographer and academic Nicos Philippou as a "key moment in the history of representing Cyprus."[9] Philippou argues that Thomson's photographs are not mere records of a particular historical moment in Cyprus, but rather that these depictions were instrumental to the colonial project in the way they became part of a specific vision of Cyprus.[10] Amidst the many photographs, Thomson's subjects are anonymous, grouped under what he perceived as generalized cultural characteristics of a decaying place – characteristics that were later reproduced by colonial officials. Philippou critiques the unquestioning reproduction of Thomson's work, suggesting that

1 "This new Scheme will Aid the Women who Fetch the Water," *Cyprus Review*, April 1, 1949, 6–7.

2 Ibid.

3 "The Men Talk but the Women Fetch the Water," *The Cypriot*, April 4, 1949, 2.

4 Gustavo Esteva, "Development," in *The Development Dictionary: A Guide to Knowledge as Power*, ed. Wolfgang Sachs (London: Zed Books, 2010 [1992]), 1–24.

5 For more on how the British used education and architecture to accomplish this end, see Michael Given, "Star of the Parthenon, Cypriot Melange: Education and Representation in Colonial Cyprus," *Journal of Mediterranean Studies* (1997): 59–82; Panayiota Pyla and Petros Phokaides, "Architecture and Modernity in Cyprus," EAHN *(Newsletter of the European Architectural History Network)* (2009): 36–49.

6 "Five-Year Economic Development Programme," address by President of the Republic Archbishop Makarios to the House of Representatives, August 21, 1961 [in Greek] (Nicosia: Republic of Cyprus Government Printing Office, 1961).

7 Willard Long Thorp, "Cyprus: Suggestions for a Development Programme," report prepared for the Government of the Republic of Cyprus (New York: UN, 1961).

it contributes to a romanticized view of the past in Cyprus while overlooking its colonial implications.[11]

More importantly, however, his criticism also applies to the reproduction and evaluation of Thomson's work by international institutions such as the UK National Archives. In an online article titled "John Thomson: Victorian Pioneer of Photojournalism," published April 17, 2020, his work is discussed without mentioning his likely association with British imperialism, let alone evaluating its effect on his work.[12]

CONFLICTING DEPICTIONS OF THE 'CYPRIAN WOMAN'

In trying to make sense of Cyprus, Thomson produced conflicting narratives, inadvertently revealing how Cyprus resisted uncomplicated categorization. A particularly interesting example is his decision to photograph women across six different plates – four of which are associated with water: "A Cyprian Maid," "A Water-carrier," "Women at the Well" and "Coming from the Well."[13] The Cypriot women are described in terms of their beauty, which is associated with ancient Greek statues and an imagined Hellenic lineage.

However, this association relies on superficial, narrowly defined features generally described as 'physiognomy' and 'type' in the nineteenth-century pseudoscience that later became the basis for 'scientific' racism.[14] In the case of colonial Cyprus, external features are used in European contexts to signify a collective character rather than an individual character.[15] Even the women's 'terracotta jars' are linked to an imagined Hellenic ancestry, since in Thomson's view they resembled those found in ancient Hellenistic tombs.[16] Although Thomson visually provides a vivid record of the close association between women and water, his images do not necessarily capture the everyday lives of Cypriot women – their socio-political role in their respective communities and individual identities. Instead, women are depicted as mute, looking away from the camera as if caught mid-motion, passively posed against white backgrounds. As such, and as Philippou also notes, the women are feminized as compared to their male Cypriot counterparts.[17]

Later, during the crucial period of late colonialism and welfare development, Sir Patrick Balfour (1904–1976) wrote:

> The predominant motives of local crime are water and women, in that order. Water means life or death, and a Cypriot will kill another more readily for interfering with his water supply, than for interfering with his wife.[18]

Balfour, Kemal Atatürk's biographer and a white, British homosexual man, provides a rather typical orientalist view of Cyprus in the 1950s. His written account is one of many about 'the orient' (others include Turkey, Egypt and Greece). Despite the orientalism characteristic of other accounts of Cyprus at the time, the above excerpt reveals not only the broader contestations over this vital resource among agrarian Cypriots, but also how water was entwined with gender identities, presenting both water and women as 'things' – objects of contention deprived of agency.

Later in his book, Balfour tries to remedy his description of Cyprus as a vastly degraded landscape and its people – especially its women – as ugly. However, he still emphasizes that, despite their redeeming qualities, they remain uncultured peasants:

> The men are worse than beasts, the women more ugly than fancy can conceive human females to be....
> As time went on, I found that the Cypriots are better-looking than the Turks, more honest than the Arabs, and more stable than the Greeks.

8 Garnet Wolseley, "Thursday 30th (July) 1878," *CYPRUS 1878: The Journal of Sir Garnet Wolseley*, ed. Anne Cavendish (Nicosia: Zavallis Litho, 1992), 22.

9 Nicos Philippou, "Between East and West: John Thomson in Cyprus," *Cyprus Review* (2013): 111–31.

10 Philippou, "Between East and West" (see note 9).

11 Philippou, "Between East and West" (see note 9).

12 Katherine Howells, *John Thomson: Victorian Pioneer of Photojournalism*, The National Archives, April 17, 2020 (blog), nationalarchives.gov.uk/john-thomson-victorian-pioneer-of-photojournalism/ (accessed October 22, 2023). In stark contrast, see the free online database by MIT OpenCourseWare, *Visualizing Cultures*, where John Thomson's photographic illustration of China is indeed explored through the lens of colonialism, orientalism and the cultural hegemony of the West: visualizingcultures.mit.edu/home/index.html (accessed March 4, 2024).

13 John Thomson, *Through Cyprus with the Camera, in the Autumn of 1878* (London: Sampson Low, Marston, Searle, Rivington, 1879).

14 For more on Victorian physiognomy see: Sharrona Pearl, *About Faces: Physiognomy in Nineteenth-Century Britain* (Boston: Harvard University Press, 2010).

15 Philippou, "Between East and West" (see note 9); Christopher Pinney, *Camera Indica/The Social Life of Indian Photographs* (London: Reaktion Books, 1997).

16 John Thomson, *Through Cyprus with the Camera* (see note 13).

17 Philippou, "Between East and West" (see note 9).

18 Patrick Balfour, *The Orphaned Realm: Journeys in Cyprus* (London: Percival Marshall, 1951).

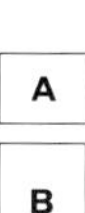

A "Kaimakli women at the fountain, for water and gossip," postcard, Kaimakli, Nicosia 1930. Photographer: Haigaz Mangoian, Source: ©The Leventis Municipal Museum of Nicosia, LMMN: /1988/131,4.

B Pyrgos Tyllirias Water Development Works, completed in 1960, designed and constructed by the WDD, Source: PIO "Water Supply and Irrigation 1950s" folder, reference no. 28A-0109-0007

> They are quite distinct from their neighbours. They are in fact, in spite of everything, Cypriots. Their history might have produced a race of slaves and bastards. It has not done so. It has produced a people, without an individual culture, but with a strong individual character, stubborn, conceited and sincere. The Cypriots, whether traders, moneylenders, lawyers, doctors or journalists, are peasants, or sons or grandsons of peasants.[19]

This ambivalent disposition towards the 'peasant Cypriot' and his ugly female counterpart, who are at once conceited and sincere, indicates a switch in mode of governmentality. This shift, aimed at repressing Greek nationalism and the concurrent expansion of water infrastructure in the aftermath of the Second World War (and continuing up to the Greek Cypriot guerrilla campaign of 1955–59), is reflected in the integration of development with welfare measures. Cyprus differs with respect to other colonized territories in that most of its people – i.e., the Greek Cypriot community – did not seek independence, but unification with Greece. While Greek Cypriot nationalism has long been associated with anti-colonialism, this is an oversimplification. In fact, the presence of Turkish Cypriots as the second largest community on the island created a complex political dynamic of exclusion. Arguably, Turkish Cypriot nationalism – which eventually climaxed in the Turkish invasion and occupation of the northern part of the island in 1974 – was inextricably linked to its Greek Cypriot counterpart. The cultural hegemony of both nationalisms, especially during the post-colonial period, still partakes of the vision of Cypriot women as black-clad, weeping wives and mothers of missing persons; this is another kind of cultural violence that extends beyond the intercommunal conflict.

A FEMINIST READING OF CYPRIOT WATER

The search for decolonial histories beyond the conventional archive is most evident in efforts to write histories of architecture and cities from a feminist, intersectional and even post-humanist perspective.[20] Efforts to explore these hidden histories, particularly through a feminist lens, are evident in Cypriot historiography. Sevina Floridou's *Stones that Whisper* delves into historical responses to death, emphasizing anthropological perspectives and folklore in Limassol.[21] She highlights the significance of graveyards and tomb inscriptions in understanding the socio-cultural significance of women's rituals, especially during the Ottoman and early British colonial periods. Among other things, this includes the exploration of specific buildings like the hammam, as well as unconventional sources such as the biographical account of the female hodja of Pir Ali Dede Tekke, Seyhinin Safye Hanum (active from 1937 until 1974).

In a similar vein, Anna Marangou collects popular stories and cross-references them with archival information and travellers' logs across the Frankish, Venetian and Ottoman periods to offer a different history of Cyprus and specifically of Nicosia. These are not stories of violence and conflict, but are rather framed around the relationships between humans and nature established with the river that so long ago used to pass through the heart of the city.[22]

Artist Kyriaki Costa's cumulative work offers a creative response to histories of water while also recording them. In a catalogue of small-scale, water-related infrastructure in Nicosia entitled *Her Water*, Costa extensively records public and private fountains and watering troughs, including modernist concrete water tanks from the colonial 1940s and post-independence 1960s.[23] By capturing these infrastructures, both Costa and Marangou recognize their significance in shaping daily life and contributing

19 Balfour, *The Orphaned Realm* (see note 18), 23–24.

20 In the recent work of architects and urbanists Despoina Stratigakos and Ioanna Theocharopoulou, diverse narratives of city, architecture and national histories emerge through innovative synthesis of new materials not necessarily found in formal archives. Despoina Stratigakos, *Where Are the Women Architects?* (New Jersey: Princeton University Press, 2016); Ioanna Theocharopoulou, *Builders, Housewives and the Construction of Modern Athens* (Onassis Foundation: Polis, [2022] 2017). From other fields of the humanities, Macarena Gómez-Barris and Farhana Sultana both highlight the impact of colonialism and extractive industries on water and Indigenous communities, emphasizing the need for a decolonial approach to water management, especially in the Global South: Macarena Gómez-Barris, *The Extractive Zone: Social Ecologies and Decolonial Perspectives* (Durham, NC: Duke University Press, 2017).

21 Sevina Floridou, *Stones That Whisper: Dervishes and Women's Rituals in Limassol* (Nicosia: Costas and Rita Severis Foundation, 2021).

22 Anna Marangou, *Perpatontas stis ochthes tou potamou Pedieou* [Walking along the banks of the Pedieos river] (Athens: Rodakio, 2018).

23 Kyriaki Costa, *Her Water* (Nicosia: Point Centre for Contemporary Art, 2016).

24 Urban catalysts are hereby understood as defined by Aldo Rossi, *The Architecture of the City* (Cambridge, MA; London: MIT Press, 1982 [1966]).

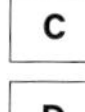

C "A water-carrier" as photographed by John Thomson, *c.* 1878, courtesy of the University of St Andrews Libraries and Museums.

D Photograph of a fountain inscribed "ER 1956," designating the year of construction and Queen Elizabeth as the benefactor of this Turkish Cypriot village in the Mesaoria plains. Source: PIO photographic archive, under the folder "Water Supply and Irrigation 1950s," reference no. 28A-0055-0002, captioned "Mora village water supply."

to the city's co-produced cultural heritage. These fountains, adorned with the inscriptions of their financiers and municipal benefactors, positioned at the centre of small squares or the entrance to main roads within the medieval city walls of Nicosia, serve as catalysts of urbanity.[24]

Accompanying Costa's work is her correspondence with the mayoral office of Nicosia, in which she calls for the maintenance of the fountains to ensure their accessibility to the public, and for the re-introduction of troughs for animals. More than just a catalogue, her project is a form of artistic activism aimed at developing a commons and infrastructures of care. Despite their obvious significance, fountains – especially in southern Nicosia – have all but vanished. This is largely due to the inter-ethnic conflict between Greek and Turkish Cypriots after independence, compounded by a longstanding, overzealous effort to de-Ottomanize the urban landscape of the capital. First introduced by the British colonizers who, under the guise of development, tried to replace this 'oriental' element with a highly compromised vision of modernity and urbanity, these concrete fountains and reservoirs are typically devoid of any ornament or cultural affiliation except the understated yet definitive colonialist imperial cypher "GR" (Georgius Rex) or "ER" (Elizabeth Regina) (**FIG. D**).

Even if it seems that aesthetics were not a priority for colonial officials who made decisions concerning these techno-political artefacts, the cast-concrete constructions nevertheless embodied a modernist aesthetic as well as an ideology linked to a host of issues: the benevolence of the welfare state in Britain; the loss of other British colonies; the island's simmering, reactionary nationalism; and the upsurge of workers' unions that eventually necessitated a series of technocratic schemes for water management. At the same time, the many photographic records of these utilitarian urban artefacts typify the established, problematic way in which architectural modernism records and presents its products. In this case, women (and children, both non-masculine presences) were used as props to convince viewers of the infrastructure's usefulness, benevolence and modernity.[25]

Material culture and iconography are highly indicative of both popular and official state colonial imagination. In the case of water, the varied records of work and progress around water management and infrastructure clearly reveal a high modernist aesthetic and ideology that has preserved colonial schemes depicting peasants being modernized by engineers. As such, these belong to an imagined, modernized state and later Hellenic nationalism, which was largely based on stereotypical depictions – including those of women performing 'womanly' domestic duties or as part of a romanticized, picturesque countryside in the process of being modernized.

These same notions are nevertheless contradicted by the paradox of Cyprus's "idiosyncratic modernity."[26] On the one hand, there is the official version, comprising meticulous reports authored by engineers and directors, maps and censuses conducted by other government agents, clerks, geologists, hydrologists and the like. On the other hand, there is an abundance of other institutional archives that, despite their descriptive titles, contain a great deal of information that is not readily available in the official written reports. For example, official reports divide workers into 'skilled' and 'unskilled' labourers to calculate their compensation, yet none of these reports contain detailed information regarding the workers' identities, the number of hours of labour needed or the knowledge and cumulative experience they had. Even compensation was not fixed, as we learn from a former Water Development Department (WDD) clerk.[27]

Despite the existence of a fixed rate by which labourers were compensated according to their skills, the apparatus devised for the construction and funding of water works had a formal and an informal component that was susceptible to abuse, ensuring that women would always fall under the unskilled category. This apparatus – and I use the word here in the Foucauldian sense to designate legislation and bodies that enforce power but also to allude to its connection to the word infrastructure itself – is a British colonial one, constructed by men and hence patriarchal. It was expected that women would not be included in official records or even in later Cypriot historiography, because most likely there were none to include, especially as engineers or members of government bodies. However, there they are in the photographs, labouring away, engaging in very different activities than performing domestic duties like cooking, cleaning or fetching potable water – they are not, as Thomson describes them, looking "like the living model of some Greek statue" – or, as in another caption, "gossiping at the fountain" (**FIG. A**).[28]

The rest of the WDD archive contrasts with photographs depicting male technocrats overseeing and measuring the flow of water, embodying a modernist ideology in which nature has been conquered and tamed for the sake of modernization.[29] The existence of a seemingly progressive Cypriot society that encourages women to participate in labour while receiving unequal pay and little or no official recognition highlights the persistence of colonial power dynamics and the contradictions within modernist technoscience.

Nevertheless, archival images of this kind enable us to witness Cypriot women as part of these strenuous processes, even subverting their popular depiction in traditional dances like the *kouza* – named after the terracotta vessel used by women to carry water and portrayed as an all-female dance based on the mythology of women gossiping and courting men at fountains (**FIG. B**).[30]

CONCLUSION

This essay has presented findings that can begin to shed light on gender inequalities relating to water as well as the spatial dynamics and cultural significance of water infrastructure in Cyprus in the colonial and post-colonial periods. These insights can inform future methodologies for studying the recent history of Cyprus in a colonial context. For instance, such approaches could integrate intersectional, ecofeminist perspectives to document women's histories, or explore the intricate political dynamics surrounding water and other infrastructures of care that extend beyond the confines of colonial governance. After examining issues regarding the nature of colonial and post-colonial development in the context of Cyprus, particularly in respect to water, a clear conclusion emerges: water infrastructures were co-produced within a negotiated modernity, a concept ripe for exploration within the extensive history of urban water management. This history includes water's legal and physical infrastructure under colonialism, revealing an enduring colonial imprint that affected different segments of the population disparately. These aspects call for further investigation. •

25 Beatriz Colomina, for example, considers these popularized depictions in mass media the real 'space' within which modernist architecture and its problematic perceptions of gender were constructed: Beatriz Colomina, *Privacy and Publicity: Modern Architecture as Mass Media* (Boston: MIT Press, 1996).

26 Elena Stylianou and Nicos Philippou, "Greek-Cypriot Locality: (Re) Defining our Understanding of European Modernity," in *A Companion to Modern Art*, ed. Pam Meecham (New Jersey: John Wiley & Sons, 2018), 339–58.

27 H. Karakannas, "The Evolution of Domestic Water Supplies and Public Health in Cyprus" (MPhil Thesis, Loughborough University, 1988).

28 Thomson, *Through Cyprus with the Camera* (see note 13).

29 Like the main character of Ayn Rand's *The Fountainhead*, burdened with the task of bettering the lives of all people.

30 This is not to diminish the value of street and square fountains as a crucial part of everyday life and socialization in Cyprus throughout the 19th and 20th centuries, up to the eventual installation of indoor plumbing, which slowly began in the late 1950s.

Bordoclima: New Calligraphies of Fluid Borders

Lucia Rebolino and Federica Pessotto challenge the notion of fixed borders within contemporary geopolitics by conceptualizing them as dynamic entities. Their approach advocates the sovereignty of water in shaping borders and proposes a fluid understanding characterized by constant change and permeability.

Lucia Rebolino,
Federica Pessotto

Bordoclima experiments with the concept of borders in modern geopolitics and environmental dynamics. Using new methods and cartographic expressions, it focuses on the idea of moving borders, recognizing the sovereignty of water and air in shaping these boundaries. By applying principles from fluid dynamics, Bordoclima transforms static borders into dynamic entities composed of fluid elements in continuous motion. These borders are categorized as two types: the liquid type, which include water bodies such as rivers, glaciers and oceans; and the gaseous type, encompassing air and the atmosphere.

In this framework, borders acquire a three-dimensional aspect characterized by dynamism, permeability and indivisibility. This approach recognizes the constant state of change and movement inherent in physical borders, akin to natural processes of water erosion and decomposition. The interaction between humans and fluid borders, especially rivers, evolves over time, reflecting the interplay of natural and artificial territorial demarcations.

These new dynamic models of borders involve the use of a new 'calligraphic' language capable of generating new aesthetic and performative forms of landscape. Ecology is seen as a science of possibilities, not as a discipline that defines definitive spatial outcomes. The tools and methods of landscape ecology are used and tested to map and simulate the movement of borders through complex software and data analysis. These critical tools can trace global and local phenomena, considering the outcome of an ecological project as a probabilistic and non-deterministic scenario.

The borders of the Balkans, as they mostly overlap with fluid bodies, become a territory of experimentation where interference and disturbance take the form of holograms representing conflict – both political and ecological.

In the "New Climatic Regime,"[1] Bordoclima challenges the traditional architectural perspective of borders as static and rigid. It proposes a paradigm in which ecological and geopolitical boundaries are in continuous fluctuation. This shift necessitates new methodological and design approaches, accommodating the fluid and ever-changing nature of borders in a world facing ecological challenges and climate crisis. •

1 Bruno Latour, *Down to Earth: Politics in the New Climatic Regime* (Cambridge, UK: Polity Press, 2018).

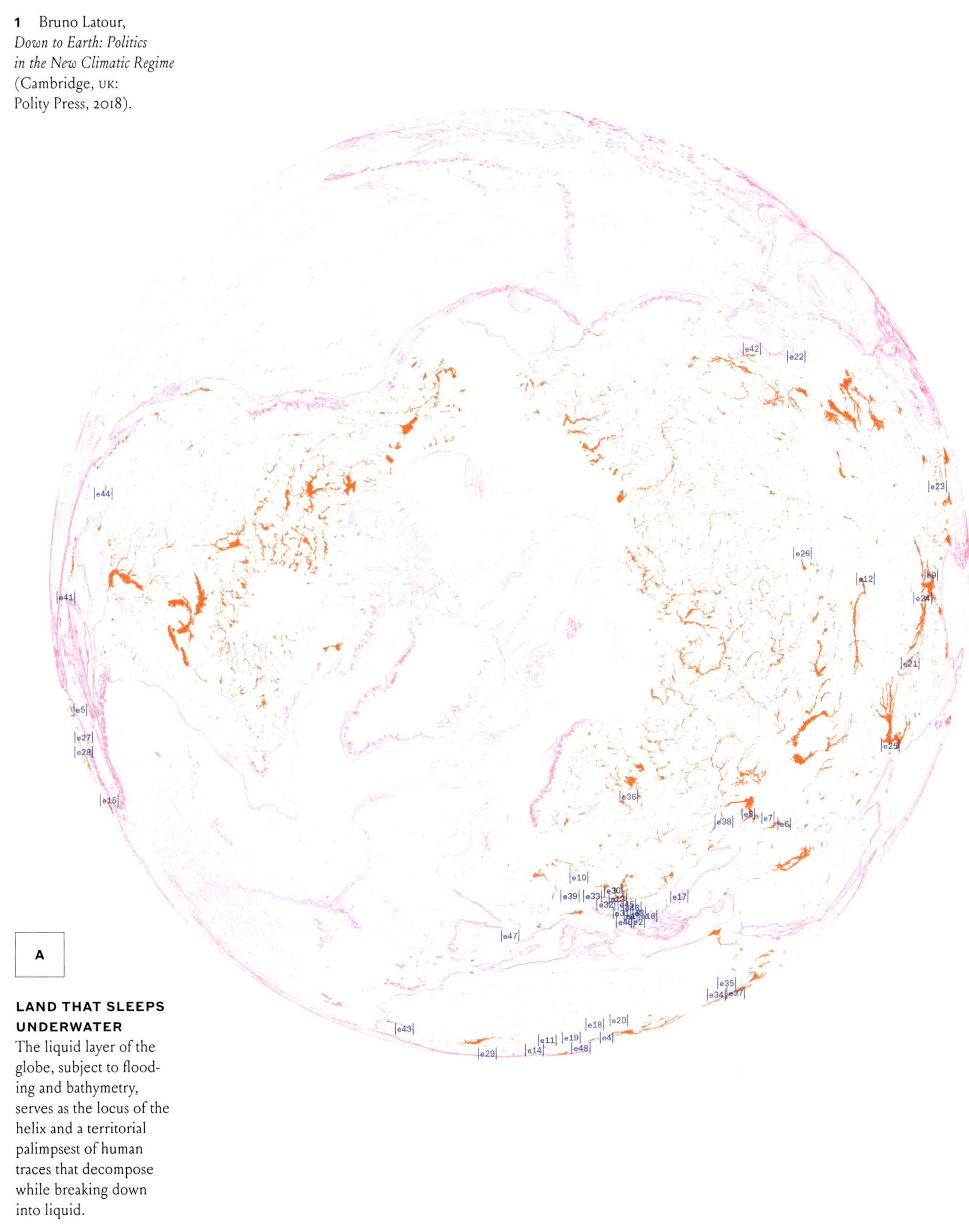

A

LAND THAT SLEEPS UNDERWATER

The liquid layer of the globe, subject to flooding and bathymetry, serves as the locus of the helix and a territorial palimpsest of human traces that decompose while breaking down into liquid.

B

C

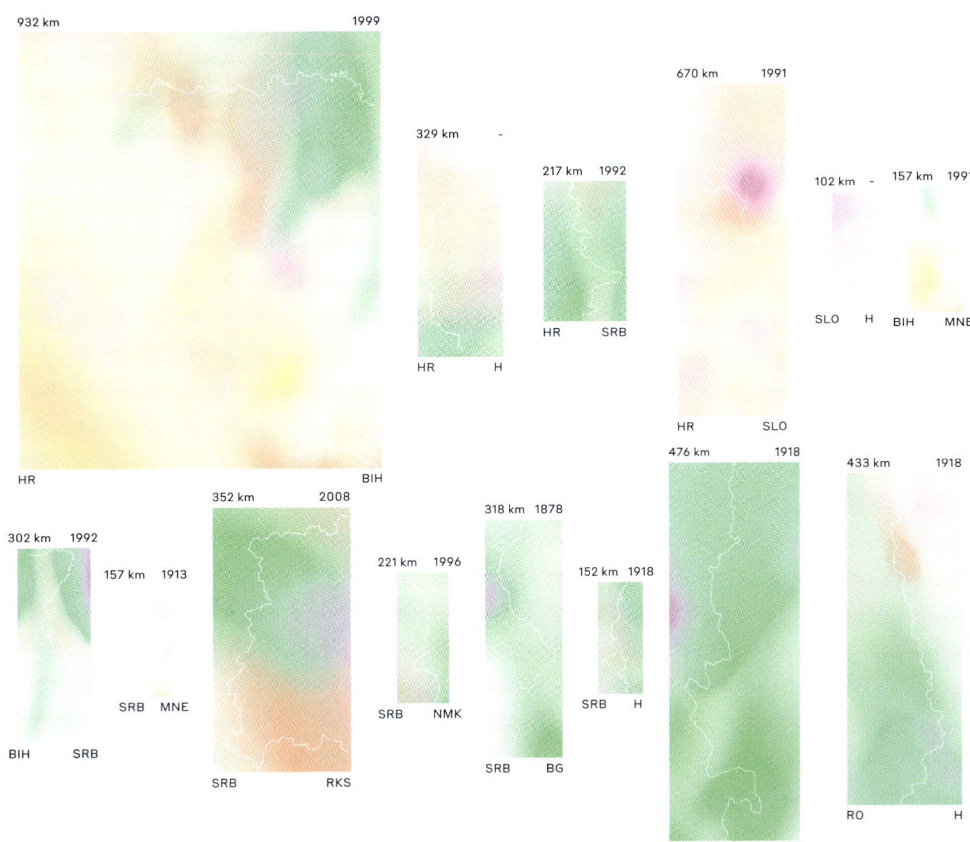

B
THE MASTER PLAN OF THE BALKANS
A mapping of ecological and social fragilities and holograms of conflict, interacting with the fluid dimension of the border. The boundary rejects linear and static logic and includes elements outside the visible geopolitical realm, such as water and air boundaries. In so doing, it introduces the concept of a fluid border on the map; related geopolitical phenomena can be traced back to graphic semiology.

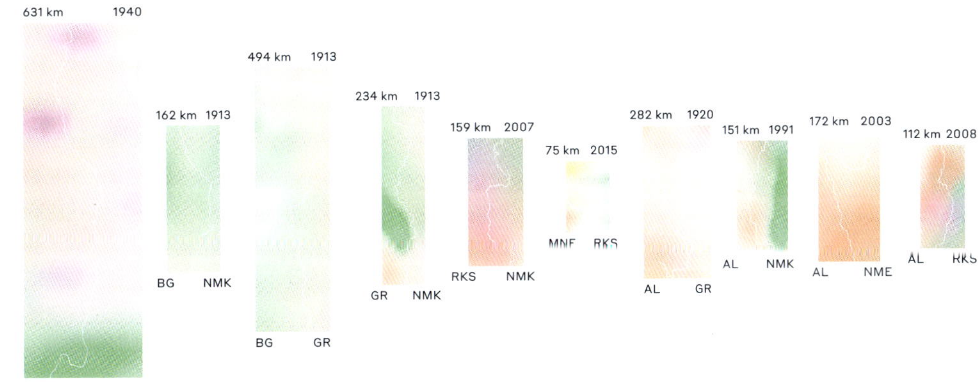

C
CARDS FROM THE ATMOSPHERE
Air borders are virtual limits in space, yet they fall under state jurisdiction and are regulated by international agreements and treaties similar to those used to govern territories. Alternative cartographies of the air can enable the modelling of its dynamics, creating future scenarios and producing alternative projects suspended in the biosphere.

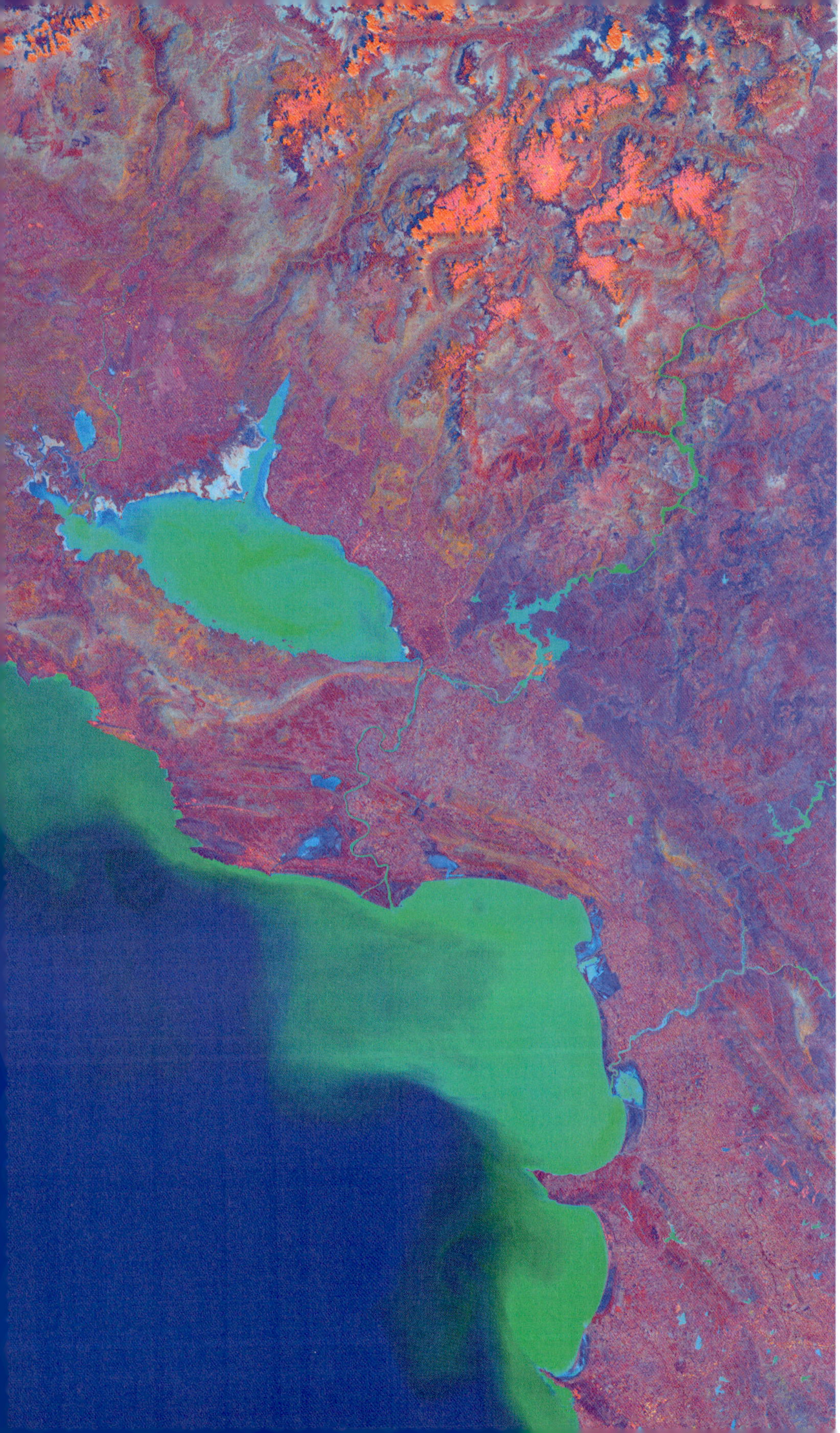

Bordoclima

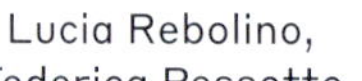

Lucia Rebolino,
Federica Pessotto

D E

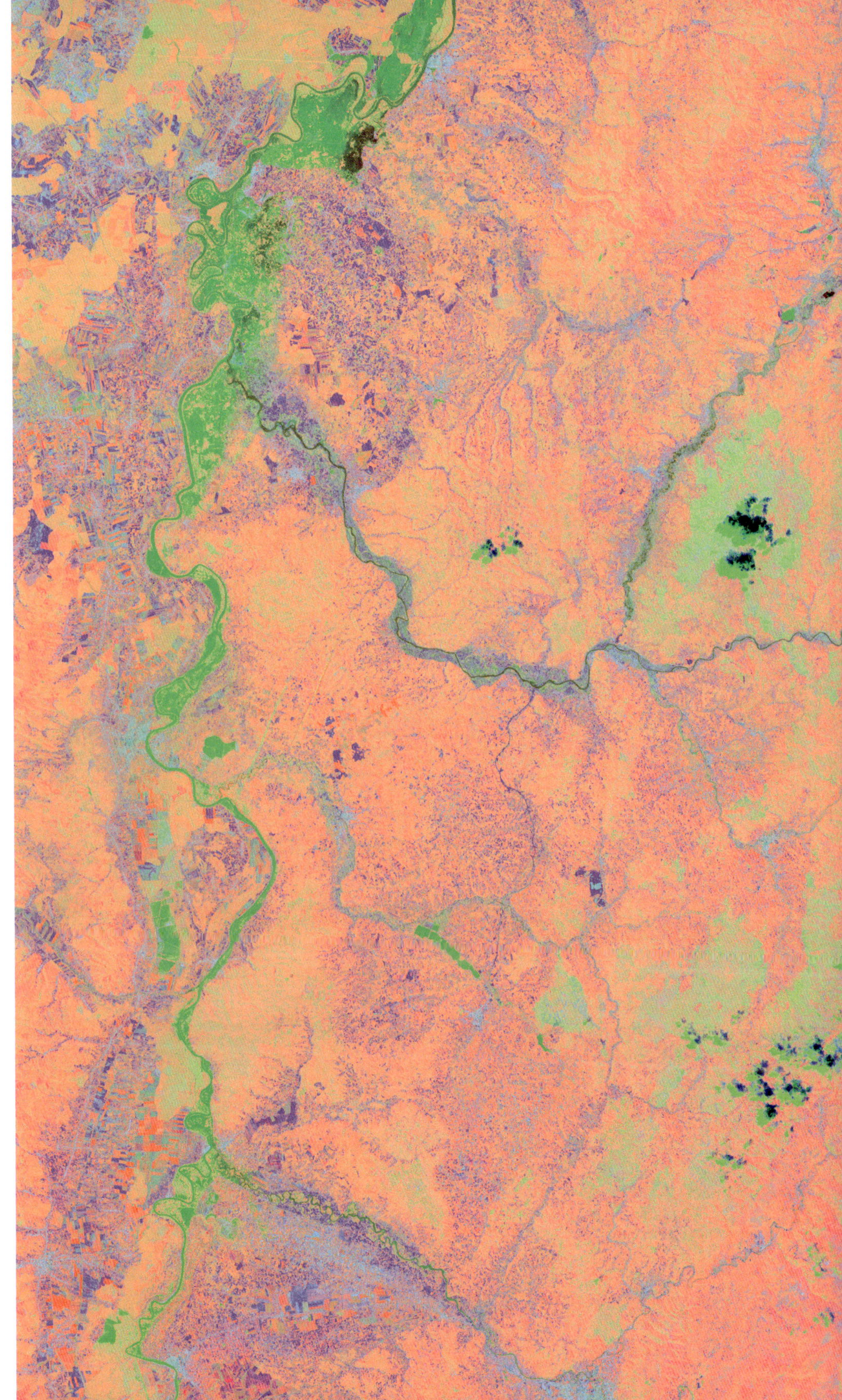

D Albania–Montenegro fluid border

E Croatia–Bosnia Herzegovina fluid border

Bordoclima

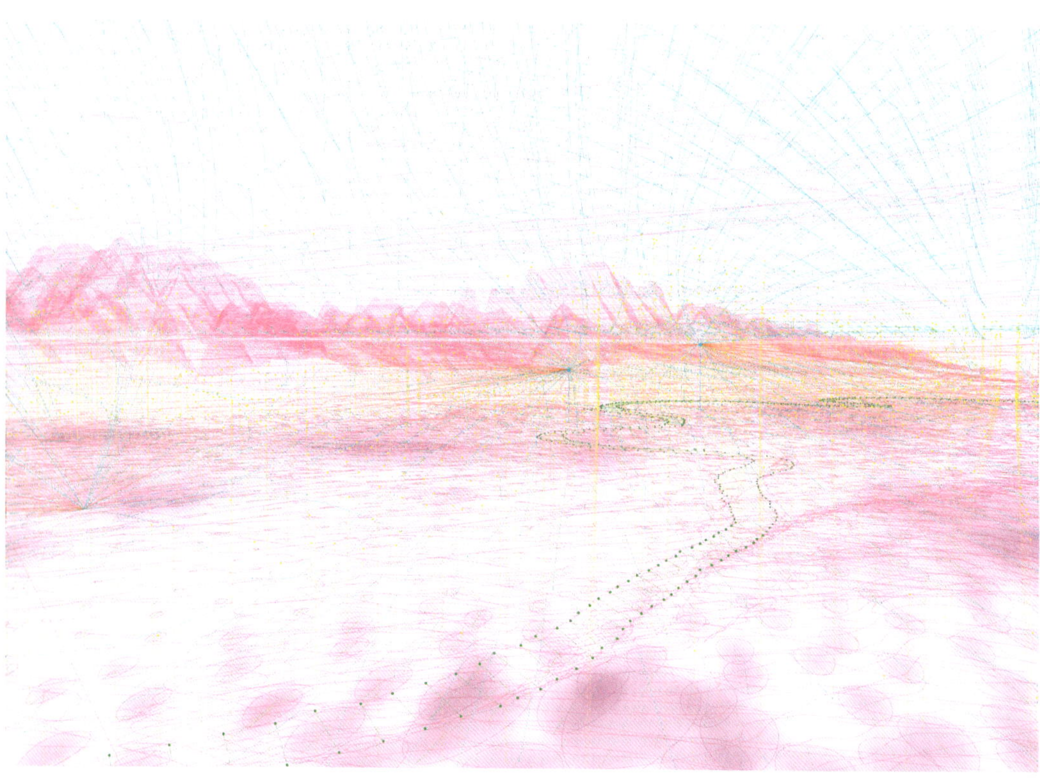

Lucia Rebolino,
Federica Pessotto

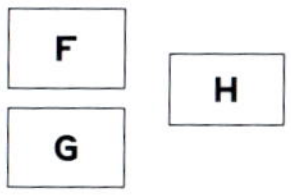

F
VELIKA KLADUSA – GLINA RIVER
The river acts as a moving ecological corridor used by migrants to travel along the border. This town, located in Bosnia, is marked by a severe migration crisis that has long affected the Balkan Route.

G
SLAVONSKI BROD – SAVA RIVER
This fragmented spot in Croatia is characterized by a hybrid fluid regime, composed of both natural liquid overflows and gas emissions from the air pollution of the old oil refinery in the Bosnian town of Bosanski Brod.

H
A NEW TOPOGRAPHY OF THE BORDER
This fragmented spot in Croatia exhibits a hybrid fluid regime, marked by overflows in both liquid and gas forms, caused by water flooding and the pervasive air pollution stemming from the old oil refinery in the Bosnian town of Bosanski Brod, which expands as a gradient over the border.

Desalination and a New Environmental Public

Linda Schilling Cuellar tackles the complexities surrounding water management in Chile, questioning the polarizing allure of desalination. She reveals the multifaceted implications of landscape solutionism – technological interventions, privatization debates and ecological repercussions. In her exploration, water emerges as a critical lifeline amidst the ever-pressing climate crisis.

Linda Schilling Cuellar

Since Chile established its first modern desalination plant in 2003, there has been a surge in the construction of such infrastructures to address water scarcity, particularly in the northern and central regions of the country, which have been impacted by a megadrought.[1] Today, there are twenty-eight desalination plants distributed along the Pacific Coast – three of them already obtained environmental approval.[2] This essay examines the rise of desalination in Chile through the lens of "landscape solutionism," analyzing what can go wrong despite extensive planning and permit approval processes.[3] In particular, the essay investigates community expectations and the communication strategy employed in a specific desalination project, drawing on the environmental impact assessment reports submitted to the Servicio de Evaluación Ambiental de la República de Chile (SEA), Chile's Environmental Evaluation Service. The case study examines a desalination plant construction process in Los Vilos, intended for industrial use by the Minera Los Pelambres, a copper mine in the Coquimbo Region. This analysis reveals that the pursuit of water within the context of extraction activities pushes ecologies to unprecedented extremes. However, it also highlights the potential for design disciplines to facilitate public participation and foster 'environmental publics' that engage with spatial and temporal dimensions of knowledge beyond the operational timeframe of desalination.[4]

A RACE AGAINST DROUGHT

To catch up with the proliferation of desalination plants, the Chilean government adopted a national water resource strategy in 2012, designating desalination as the proposed solution to address water scarcity. The strategy states that "To expedite the processing of the permits and authorizations related to these kinds of projects, a review of the protocols that apply to their development will also be conducted."[5] As a result, in April 2023 the SEA drafted a guide for the description of desalination plant projects.[6] While the government rushes to keep up with the rise of desalination plant projects, industry coalesces around organizations like the Latin American Association of Desalination and Water Reuse (ALADYR), created in 2010, and the Associación Chilena de Desalinación y Reúso A.G. (ACADES), created in 2021; the latter promotes the "improvement of policies and regulations for the reuse and desalination industries through scientific evidence and national and international experience."[7] Both government and industry mobilize a public message in which desalination is presented as a sustainable and feasible solution to water needs for people and industries alike. This message does not clearly convey that it is primarily the industrial sector that benefits from this technology, with eighty percent of facilities allocating their water production for use in mining and industrial processes.[8]

The general proposition of turning to the ocean for water by reversing the water cycle – a new development made possible by reverse osmosis technologies – goes uncontested for a long, narrow country like Chile. Government and industry in this geographical context perceive water scarcity as an issue too complex to frame and solve; therefore, both resort to short-term fixes by addressing the lack of water through desalination in a move characteristic of what landscape architect Rob Holmes identifies as "landscape solutionism" or "the recurring temptation to see landscape design through the prism of known solutions."[9] With Chile's 6 435 kilometres of coastline, it is easy to view the vastness of the Pacific Ocean as a reservoir for a resource that has quickly become scarce, leading to expectations for engineering to devise solutions to keep business as usual.

ENGINEERING CRISES

Reliance on engineering to address problems posited by the landscape comes from a long history of economic development that views nature as a resource, originating from the forceful economic exchanges between a colony and its empire. In the pursuit of profit, no feat is impossible.

As the world's leading exporter of copper, Chile has witnessed the mining industry pioneering engineering solutions that deliberately alter landscapes. With the Andes mountains and their rich mineral clusters on one side and a geographical narrowness that allows for proximity to the Pacific Ocean on the other, Chile's geography becomes a competitive advantage, allowing extraction activities to place resources on maritime routes expediently.[10] Furthermore, many of these operations rely on other landscape features, such as valleys and plains, to deposit mining by-products, such as tailings, and sterile dumps consisting of blasted rocks. These sites, referred to by legislation as 'environmental legacies' or 'environmental liabilities,' are shaping environs for centuries to come. They constitute anthropogenic landscapes with some degree of toxicity that causes an everlasting impact on the environment, and they are no accident: these terrain features are intentionally designed by global engineering firms with offices in Santiago de Chile. Lesser-discussed problems associated with these sites include: water mismanagement issues (stemming from the involvement of numerous regulating agencies in water governance and the underlying problems of water allocation as dictated by the water code);[11] the unintended consequences these operations have on coastal marine ecosystems; the impacts on local sustenance economies where intake and discharge pipelines are located;[12] and their link to the recurring climatic causes of the megadrought affecting the country since 2010.[13] In addition to these issues, present-day desalination practices differ from historical practices, which manipulated the water cycle. These practices, which date back to Inca irrigation systems and the *acequias* [irrigation ditches] employed by Spanish settler colonies, involve reversing the conventional water cycle, which typically flows from the Andes to the Pacific Ocean. This unassuming process for securing a new source of water in places

1 René D. Garreaud, Juan P. Boisier, Roberto Rondanelli, Aldo Montecinos, Hector H. Sepúlveda and Daniel Veloso Aguila, "The Central Chile Mega Drought (2010–2018): A Climate Dynamics Perspective," *International Journal of Climatology* 40, no. 1 (January 2020): 421–39.

2 Associación Chilena de Desalinación y Reúso A.G. (ACADES) et al., "Primer Catastro Nacional de Plantas y Proyectos de Desalinización en Chile," April 2023, acades.cl/proyectos/.

3 Rob Holmes, "The Problem with Solutions," *Places Journal* (July 2020).

4 Lesley Green, "Ecology, Race, and the Making of Environmental Publics: A Dialogue with Silent Spring in South Africa," *Resilience: A Journal of the Environmental Humanities* 1, no. 2 (2014); Shela Sheikh, "The Future of the Witness: Nature, Race and More-than-Human Environmental Publics," *Kronos* 44, no. 1 (2018).

5 Dirección General de Aguas (DGA) and Gobierno de Chile, "Estrategia Nacional de Recursos Hídricos 2012–2025."

6 SEA, "Guía para la descripción de proyectos de plantas desalinizadoras en el SEIA," (Gobierno de Chile, 2023).

7 Website of the Associación Chilena de Desalinación y Reúso A.G. (ACADES), "About Us," congresoacades. cl/about-us/ (accessed April 8, 2024).

dependent on mining and agriculture – the main economic activities of national interest – stresses a 'landscape solutionist' approach that lacks the foresight to reflect on the spatial implications of such solutions for local communities and ecologies.

THE UNINTENDED CONSEQUENCES OF SOLUTIONS

Landscape solutionism as described by Holmes presents three interlinked dynamics that together constitute the basis for unintended negative consequences as observed in desalination construction practices. Taking as a case study the construction of a desalination plant in Los Vilos intended for industrial use by Minera Los Pelambres, a copper mine in the Coquimbo Region, this section unpacks these three dynamics.[14]

Firstly, landscape solutionism overlooks the fact that certain aspects of the landscape are socially and ecologically important, but not necessarily problematic. In 2004, the Conchalí Lagoon, situated on land owned by the mine in Los Vilos, was designated as a Ramsar site, aimed at conserving and sustainably using wetlands.[15] The mine assumed stewardship of the wetlands, seeking to control foraging practices that were perceived as a primary threat, despite upstream activities further compromising this fragile ecosystem.[16] This conservation effort estranged locals from their environment, reflecting power imbalances entrenched in extraction activities and local communities. Visitors now access the wetland area via pedestrian trails or the Centro Andrónico Luksic Abaroa (CALA), which promotes responsible industrial mining practices.[17] However, eighteen years later, a jack-up platform used for positioning desalination plant pipelines was stranded by strong tides near the lagoon, prompting the mine to navigate bureaucratic obstacles for its removal. To avoid impacting the Ramsar area, mine workers constructed a road through the dunes and beaches, near important archaeological sites and with minimal demarcation, thereby estranging locals even further.[18] The mine identified foraging as a problem for lagoon management because it interfered not only with a fragile ecosystem, but also with their policy of maintaining 'pristine' sites near their operational areas that spoke to the mines' commitment to ecological responsibility. The pursuit of nature conservation by a qualified few – through whom science speaks – to the exclusion of locals later became a problem, as pedestrianized access constituted a new obstacle to the use of compact tractors.

A second approach characteristic of landscape solutionism involves identifying everything as a problem for which there is a known solution. Addressing water scarcity as a problem for which desalination is the solution defaults to searching for answers in already explored responses provided by markets whose interest is profit, not issue framing. Facing scarcity as an opportunity to build businesses and expand entrepreneurship is not new. The Chilean government adopted a market approach when, under the dictatorship of Augusto Pinochet, the 1981 water code privatized water rights in the name of unbiased technocratic efficiency, creating a market out of thin air in which these water rights could be bought and sold. The assumption was that private interest would implement technology-efficient systems to administer water resources in a competitive market setting. Academia and government have acknowledged this to be problematic and eventually untrue due to the impossibility of revoking water rights, which has resulted in negative trends such as speculation and inactive markets; the difficulty of enforcing water allocation quotas (since water infrastructures can be as discreet as hoses distributing water from wells hiding in plain sight); and the many regulatory bodies involved in water governance, which make accountability difficult to trace.[19] Relying on established market solutions for water scarcity – such as desalination – overshadows the underlying structural issues that impact livelihoods along the transect traversed by the mine. These structural challenges often necessitate changes in sustenance practices and, ultimately, in land-use patterns.

The third approach Holmes identifies in landscape solutionism is an unwillingness to engage with unsolvable problems or to classify these as solvable. The environmental impact assessment conducted in 2018 for the desalination plant project failed to acknowledge potential accidents linked to the use of jack-up platforms, a type of buoyant infrastructure used in the construction of off-shore maritime works. The environmental impact assessment did not list an accident involving the platform as a possibility, nor did the company address such accidents in response to comments filed by citizens of the community of Los Vilos at citizen participation meetings.[20] Despite environmental legislation allowing for locals who have situated knowledge of their environment to submit concerns and questions during the online and in-person citizen participation activities, these are often ignored. Another aspect of the desalination plants' future functioning that the mine regards as a non-issue relates to the by-product of such operations. Desalinating water through reverse osmosis produces brine – water with a high salt concentration. Brine, in this case, is dumped back into the ocean; this increases the salinity of water in the area near the discharge pipeline, affecting the surrounding marine ecology. Other concerns voiced by citizens relate to the larvae caught by the meshes in the intake pipeline, which affects the overall presence of certain key species in coastal marine ecosystems that fishermen rely on for sustenance. Along with these concerns, locals labour under the misconception that this water is destined for human consumption. These potential and future situations barely

8 Eduardo Baeza, "Plantas Desaladoras en Chile" (Asesoría Técnica Parlamentaria, May 2022).

9 Holmes, "The Problem with Solutions" (see note 3), section 4 para 1.

10 Opposite the region of Coquimbo in Chile, we find the San Juan Province on the Argentinian side, where mining has not developed at the scale of its Chilean counterpart due to the expansive Pampa that separates the Argentinian Andes and the Atlantic Ocean, making extraction and shipping much more expensive.

11 Manuel Prieto, María Christina Fragkou and Matías Calderón, "Water Policy and Management in Chile," in *Encyclopaedia of Water*, ed. Patricia Maurice, 1st ed. (Hoboken, NJ: Wiley, 2019), 1–11.

12 Sebastián Vicuña, Linda Daniele, Laura Farías, Humberto González, Pablo A. Marquet, Rodrigo Palma-Behnke and Alejandra Stehr, "Desalinización: Oportunidades y Desafíos para Abordar la Inseguridad Hídrica en Chile" (Chile: Comité Asesor Ministerial Científico sobre Cambio Climático; Ministerio de Ciencia, Tecnología, Conocimiento e Innovación, 2022).

13 The current mega-drought is the longest on record, with very few parallels observed during previous millennia; Garreaud et al., "The Central Chile Mega Drought (2010–2018)" (see note 1).

14 London Mining Network, "In the Valley of the Shadow of Death? A Report on Antofagasta Plc, Minera Los Pelambres and Caimanes," May 2017, londonminingnetwork.org/2017/05/antofagasta-chile-report/ (accessed August 5, 2024).

15 As established under the terms of the Ramsar Convention on wetlands under the auspices of UNESCO in 1971.

16 Manuel F. Contreras, Fernando Novoa and Juan Pablo Rubilar, "Lake Conchalí Ramsar Site (Laguna Conchalí, Sitio Ramsar): Chile," in *The Wetland Book II: Distribution, Description and Conservation*, ed. C. Max Finlayson, G. Randy Milton, R. Crawford Prentice and Nick C. Davidson (Dordrecht: Springer Netherlands, 2016), 1–8.

17 See centrocala.cl (accessed August 5, 2024).

18 César A. Méndez and Donald G. Jackson, "Ocupaciones Humanas del Holoceno Tardío en Los Vilos (IV Región, Chile): Origen y Características Conductuales de la Población Local de Cazadores Recolectores de Litoral," *Chungará (Arica)* 36, no. 2 (July 2004).

19 In their book *El negocio del agua: Cómo Chile se convirtió en tierra seca* [Water Business: Or How Chile Became a Dry Land] (Santiago: EDICIONES B, 2019), investigative journalist Tania Tamayo Grez and Alejandra Carmona López describe the lack of oversight from different water-governing bodies and the entanglements of the political class with these newly created water markets, which have exacerbated water stresses through intensive agribusiness; see also Prieto, Fragkou and Calderón, "Water Policy and Management in Chile" (see note 11).

20 For example, although seven citizens voiced concerns in the citizen participation process for the Proyecto de Adaptación Operacional [Operational Adaptation Project] – the last phase for environmental approval to increase desalination plant capacity – between July and October 2021, the mine did not anticipate the possibility of a jack-up platform failure until it happened in August 2022. A year later, a new exceptional addendum was added to the mine records at the SEA, indicating contingency plans and communication strategies in the event of an accident, obtaining final approval in October 2023.

A

NEXT SPREAD
Stranded auxiliary platform for positioning the desalination plant's intake and discharge pipelines belonging to Minera Los Pelambres, Los Vilos, Chile. Photo: Linda Schilling Cuellar, August 2023.

register as concerns for the mine, making evident the unwillingness to engage with the known impacts and expectations of these infrastructures.[21]

MOVING BEYOND SOLUTIONIST LANDSCAPES TOWARDS SITES OF UNKNOWABILITY

When accounting for ecosystem disturbances during the construction phases of the desalination plant, the environmental impact assessment report submitted to the SEA diligently lists all species present in a certain area as objects to be captured and relocated elsewhere, away from the mine's activities, and subsequently monitored for success indicator compliance. Instead of seeing different species as participants in relational processes modified by extraction, this framing disregards and disrupts those relational processes by shifting species around. Additionally, the commutative property of mathematics does not translate well to environmental impact assessment measures of mitigation, reparations and compensation. When filing for the initial desalination plant permits associated with the Proyecto de Infraestructura Complementaria [Additional Infrastructure Project] in 2018, only minor disturbances during the construction phase were acknowledged. These were dismissed as "low non-significant" due to industrial facilities belonging to the mine that were already in place. Furthermore, the dynamic nature of the ocean was cited as a reason for its ability to quickly rebound. Notably, no failures related to the jack-up platform were even considered.[22]

Desalination infrastructures, both during construction and operation, unleash challenges unknown to science and designers alike. Resisting the urge to operate under the framework of landscape solutionism raises the possibility of designing for what Noortje Marres calls "issue formation"– the process by which the public involves itself in politics.[23] Doing so would allow environmental controversies – such as those emerging from desalination sites linked to tensions between socio-technical arrangements and the environment – to be explored as sites of unknowability. This provides the opportunity to meet issues not with a solutionist approach, but with a spirit of inquiry in order to identify emergent relationships produced by these new processes. In addressing environmental controversies as spaces for issue formation, a new sphere of stakeholders can be shaped from individuals with spatial and temporal relationships that exceed the timeline of the desalination plant's operations and manifest themselves in citizen participation processes. Despite problems of representation and access to citizen participation meetings, these are windows into the environmental impact assessment evaluation process that allow for contestation at an institutional level. These, in turn, could be leveraged to understand the nuances of individuals who do not see themselves represented in mass environmental movements and have concerns about how these activities will impact their surroundings, and in some cases their livelihoods. This was the case for a number of associations of fishermen, miners and farmers along the Choapa Valley in the Coquimbo Region when submitting comments in the most recent citizen participation process. These environmental controversies have the potential to bring what Leslie Green refers to as an "environmental public" back into the spatial realm. In other words, by restoring what engineering has erased and nature conservation practices have removed: an environmentally-minded public that understands nature not as something 'out there' ruled by government and science – or in this case industry – but as something in which all participate.[24] Therefore, when working in and around areas of socio-environmental conflict where extractive activities take place, design disciplines have much to contribute in recognizing practices that register environmental change, many of which are disregarded as marginal livelihoods (like fishing and shellfish collecting), as well as in designing with public involvement in mind.[25]

CONCLUSION

The spatial implications of an accident involving an auxiliary platform for the maritime works required of a desalination plant in Chile reveal an underlying landscape solutionist approach that prioritizes the interests of capital by addressing the water needs of economic activities rather than those of humans. Arguing for environmental controversies as sites of unknowability, by contrast, favours harnessing citizen participation processes triggered by environmental impact assessments as sites for fostering environmental publics. There is much to engage with regarding new relationships between communities and these burgeoning socio-technical arrangements, which demand a new form of political engagement to which designers should attend. Many other areas of extraction activities remain unseen, thus avoiding public scrutiny and keeping environmental controversies out of the public eye. Engaging an environmental public in these sites of unknowability allows for the documentation of relationships through livelihoods affected by environmental change, which is crucial for understanding the changes triggered by technology-driven interventions – in this case, the desalination plant. •

21 Argyris Panagopoulos and Katherine-Joanne Haralambous, "Environmental Impacts of Desalination and Brine Treatment – Challenges and Mitigation Measures," *Marine Pollution Bulletin* 161 (December 2020): 111773.

22 Jaime Illanes y Asociados, "Estudio de Impacto Ambiental Proyecto Infraestructura Complementaria. Capitulo 4: Predicción y Evaluación Del Impacto Ambiental" (Minera Los Pelambres, 2016).

23 Noortje Marres, "The Issues Deserve More Credit: Pragmatist Contributions to the Study of Public Involvement in Controversy," in *Social Studies of Science* 37, no. 5 (October 2007): 759–80.

24 Green, "Ecology, Race" (see note 4).

25 As recently as February 1, 2024, changes introduced in SEA regulations move in that direction. Modifications to comply with the Escazú Agreement – Regional Agreement on Access to Information, Public Participation and Justice in Environmental Matters in Latin America and the Caribbean – demand that all project managers submit an Environmental Impact Assessment (EIA) that includes participatory monitoring. The project manager has a mandate to involve the community in monitoring the phases of development of a project through the delivery of information, reports, measurements, training, coordination of field visits or others, in any of its phases. This requirement expands citizen participation processes and opens the possibility of engaging with environmental controversies and fostering environmental publics through the design of spatial arrangements. The mine is currently working on a new EIA submission to extend operations from 2037 to 2051, afforded by the inauguration of the desalination plant on March 21, 2024. This new EIA submission will have to comply with the regulations involving participatory monitoring, and so the question remains: How can design disciplines help shape this new political category?

Dam Circumsonic

Oskar Frederick Johanson delves into the sonic environment of Warragamba Dam, a metaphor for broader water management issues in Australia. Through the lens of the Dyarubbin/Hawkesbury-Nepean watershed, embodied by the dam, he reveals the melodious yet dissonant complexities of controlling water amidst colonial legacies, urbanization pressures and environmental risks.

Oskar Frederick Johanson

When the gates of Warragamba Dam (1948–1960) (**FIG. A**) are opened, the building makes noise – an unyielding, terrifying, infrasonic roar. By one account, the effect of this noise, too deep for the human ear to perceive, is best experienced on the dam's deck, directly above the coursing water, in a kind of inversion of the 'Friedrichesque' mountain vista. There, it is felt within one's marrow, as vibration, as the whole dam can be felt to move.

Though it occurs rarely, and though no one bar a handful of dam staff will ever experience it, thinking about this sound nonetheless allows us some notion of an otherwise insensible object – the Dyarubbin/Hawkesbury-Nepean watershed, the single most important hydrological structure on the east coast of Australia.[1] In its wordlessness there is captured the hydro-spatial, circumsonic[2] issues of contemporary Australia: the weight of its cities on the earth;[3] the irreconcilability of colonial structures and Indigenous ontologies; the megastructural architectures built to detain, redirect, modulate and defend against water, to geographically and temporally redistribute risk across a territory; and the 'unimaginable causality' of water and our entanglement within it.[4] Decoding these signals begins with an appraisal of the dam itself, including its hydrolithic context, its architectural forerunners and the conditions under which it was imagined and built.

OOZE AND STONE

Any analysis of the dam must begin with what are sometimes thought to be the edges of Sydney: the intersection of the Cumberland Plain – the shallow basin that contains most of the city and its old agricultural lands – with the rugged terrain that surrounds it, including the ranges of the Blue Mountains towards the west and the Illawarra Escarpment and Nepean ranges towards the south and east. Each of these ranges, which are uplifted plateaus rather than true mountains, are formed from the same sandstone bed that runs beneath the city.

Since the colony's beginning, this material has been cut into and craned away to make way for docks and streets; it has been quarried and shaped into blocks and finished with bush

1 Thinking territory through sound as an index has attracted much critical scholarship. See in particular the work of AM Kanngieser on sonic colonialities; Susan Schuppli's 'Learning from Ice' project; Taylor Coyne's enjoinment to practice deep listening to water in "Listen Deep to Subterranean Kinfrastructures," *Swamphen: A Journal of Cultural Ecology* (ASLEC-ANZ) 9 (2023); and Sophia Roosth's "Infrasonic History of the Twentieth Century," *Resilience: A Journal of the Environmental Humanities* 5, no. 3 (2018): 109–24, on the tension between sound, noise, vibration and the boundaries of sensibility.

2 Circumsonic in this sense meaning a source of a sound (L. *sonus*) that is all around, or without centre (L. *circum*).

3 For further work on the weight of cities, see Territorial Agency and, in particular, Jan Zalasiewicz, Mark Williams, Colin N. Waters, Anthony D. Barnosky, John Palmesino, Ann-Sofi Rönnskog, Matt Edgeworth et al., "Scale and Diversity of the Physical Technosphere: A Geological Perspective," *The Anthropocene Review* 4, no. 1 (2016).

4 Max Haiven, "The Dammed of the Earth," in *Rīvus: A Glossary of Water,* ed. Jose Roca and Juan Francisco Salazar (Sydney: Biennale of Sydney Limited, 2022), 121.

The gates and dam wall of Warragamba Dam, 2023. Photo: Oskar Johanson.

hammers to face the walls of the colony's various spiritual headquarters; it has been ground into and blasted away to make the city's dendritic traffic tunnel system. More recently, it has been CNC-routed and hung on brackets to clad the city's most expensive buildings in a new, vernacular turn and shaped into large logs and arranged to recall pre-industrial shorelines.[5]

The sand of this sandstone was laid down in the delta of a monolithic river many times larger than the Amazon during the Triassic Era, before the proto-Australian continent broke away from the ruins of Gondwana.[6] Capped by basalt and shales, a section of it was uplifted 200 million years ago before being worked into by water and wind to give the ranges their current form. In her own sonic metaphor, Delia Falconer has called this material the "base note" of Sydney; but, to the extent we affix to Sydney a lithic identity, the spread of its base note suggests a much broader and deeper entity than that which is captured by administrative or popularly imagined boundaries.[7]

Water laid down this stone; water yet flows over and within it. Even weeks after big rains have departed, Sydney sandstone will weep water where it is topped by a swamp or heath; oozing between beards of algae and bracken, tea-stained by angophoras, bubbling where detergent and rat shit and oil has leeched. Where it faces the sea, the stone has been gouged and fluted; it has crumbled and sagged and broken off in blocks. On the floor of the plain, the water gathers in countless wending streams. The largest of these is known by Dharug speakers as Dyarubbin, and by its colonial name, the Hawkesbury-Nepean.

This river rises as the Nepean in the ranges to the south of the plain before heading north, converging with other streams such as the Bargo and Cataract until reaching the gorge at Gulguer, where it has worked a deep cut through the sandstone. From there, it runs in the interface zone between the Blue Mountains and the plain, where the uplifted sandstone bedrock bends back beneath the surface and the gravel beds begin. Where it meets the Grose River, the river changes one of its names, becoming the Hawkesbury (while remaining Dyarubbin), before coursing on beyond the northern reach of the plain, arcing eastward and discharging into the broad, calm ria of Broken Bay. With this form, the river completely encircles the metropolis of Sydney.

The size of the river and its tributaries dwarfs that of the Burramatta/Parramatta, the much smaller river of eels, which meets Sydney Harbour where it narrows. So, although the harbour is foundational to the Sydney imaginary, it is the Dyarubbin/Hawkesbury-Nepean watershed upon which the city's destiny depends. It is this structure from which the city draws almost all of its freshwater; this structure whose many tributaries have been dammed and channelized since the start of colonization in the late eighteenth century; this structure whose floodplains have been developed into housing, and which, during big rains, floods to the devastation of millions of dollars.

At the edge of the mountains, both the uplift of the sandstone and the course of the river might at first seem to deepen the sense of a boundary: of an end to the cultural and urban fabric of Sydney; of a limit to a thing properly called a city. Local government boundaries, with all their attendant policies and maps, cleave to the river's form. But rivers and stone do not think of themselves as an edge; they do not care for the arcifinity in whose employ they often find themselves.[8] A river draws on waters from either side of its banks indiscriminately; stone warps according to deep time. These elements are the centres of their worlds, their coordinates in a slow but constant state of flux, as the plates are hauled onwards by subduction and the atmosphere swells and billabongs calve and wither.

Beginning in the late nineteenth century, as earlier water sources became exhausted, the tributaries of the Dyarubbin/Hawkesbury-Nepean watershed were sequentially dammed and weired by the colony. One after another, cyclopean works were built into the Cataract, the Avon, the Cordeaux, and the Nepean itself; the spaces behind each river atrophied by massing water, the rock beneath them creaking with unthinkable compaction.

In justifying this scheme in an address in 1885, Edward Orpen Moriarty, Engineer-in-Chief of Harbours and Rivers, began by first deriding the country the dams were to disrupt:

> The country above [the dams for the] most part is a barren plateau of the Sydney sandstone formation, sparsely clothed with a stunted vegetation of eucalyptus, Epacridaceae, and Proteaceae ... it is utterly unfit for agricultural purposes, and must ever remain so by reason of its irreclaimable barrenness. It is equally useless for pastoral purposes – [it] is, in fact, destitute of every quality which could render it fit for the occupation or habitation of man....

But, as Moriarty went on, the country's destitution did not make it useless. In fact, it stood to serve the colony in a new way, because:

> [A]s a gathering ground for a water supply it is perfection; the numerous and extensive swamps, so favourably situated to catch every coast shower, perform the twofold purposes of reservoirs and filters in the deep rocky gorges; where the streams unite evaporation and absorption are reduced to a minimum, and, while there is nothing to contaminate, the whole conditions to which it is exposed are most favourable to the purification and thorough aeration of the water.[9]

Moriarty's statement is paradigmatic of the construction and imposition of settler-colonial space in territories such as Australia.[10] That the ranges above the Nepean and its tributaries were part of a deep and entangled story with its First Nations custodians was no cause for an alternative form of value, to be considered but ultimately set aside; their story is absent entirely from any calculation; their meaning infra-sensible. In their place was a confected wilderness, that cousin of 'waste'; a kind of space that might remain nominally as it was but which, as Tracey Banivanua Mar says, must ultimately "earn its keep."[11] In the context of Australia, of course, the idea that this Country was wild in the sense of being unworked, or without use to human beings, was a fantasy.[12] As Marcia Langton, Bruce Pascoe and Bill Gammage have all argued, few parts of the continent were not in some way both cared for and modified according to First Nations lore, "managed, cultivated, named, mapped, sung and known."[13] Only very recently have these practices found wider appreciation, and, as recent plans for the watershed have proven, have yet to seriously disrupt hydro-engineering logic – despite language to the contrary.

Complementing the principal works of the Upper Nepean dams was a sprawling apparatus of pipes, pumping stations and weirs, which collected the water and channelled it to a central reservoir at the centre of the plain. From there, the water was redirected to the city, mixing with oats and flour, shit and sawdust, passing through the bodies of the city's citizens and their animals and irrigating the gardens of the governor in a kind of new, metropolitan delta.

But supporting this wider concrete architecture was a legal framework, too: a government proclamation on July 13, 1923, in the Government Gazette, declaring that the dam's combined watersheds, or catchments, were henceforth protected. It is striking that in this proclamation, after a general statement and a

5 See also the shoreline of Barangaroo, where in the 20th century massive docks erased the old sandstone cliffs, and in the 21st century, new development associated with a casino has attempted to restore their shape.

6 Tim Flannery, *The Birth of Sydney* (Melbourne: Text Publishing, 2000), 8.

7 Delia Falconer, *Sydney*, The New South Cities Series 3 (Sydney: NewSouth, 2010), 3.

8 See, for example, Ifor Duncan and Stefanos Levidis, "Weaponizing a River," *e-flux Architecture*, 2020, e-flux.com/architecture/at-the-border/325751/weaponizing-a-river/ (accessed August 6, 2024), on the concept of 'arcifinious' borders: a term taken from law that describes elements of the earth system such as mountains or rivers around or along which national and other administrative boundaries calcify.

9 Engineer-in-Chief of Harbours and Rivers Edward Orpen Moriarty's report to the Water Commission, quoted in "The Upper Nepean Scheme," *Sydney Morning Herald*, Saturday, May 9, 1885.

10 We can also imagine that Moriarty was speaking to pastoralists and squatters who might have had an eye on the land.

11 Tracy Banivanua Mar, "National Parks and the Unsettling of Emptied Lands," in *Making Settler Colonial Space Perspectives on Race, Place and Identity: On the Confection of Wilderness*, ed. idem and Edmonds Penelope

salute to the king, the exact boundaries of the catchment area are given in full, listed in an almost mindless chain of pre-computational geodata. Country reduced to landscape, landscape reduced to chains and bearings.

Not even a year before the Nepean dam was complete, a drought began that was to be the worst in colonial memory. The waters behind the Upper Nepean dams fell and the limits of the scheme were made plain. But plans for another dam, on the Warragamba River at the end of the Burragorang Valley, had been circulating the offices of the Water Board for decades; indeed dreams of it had visited the colony since its first days.[14] The river itself was a relatively short and minor tributary of the Dyarubbin/Hawkesbury-Nepean, but behind it stretched a vast theoretical space, a terrific void of the hydrological imagination. The necessary size and associated risks of this dam had hitherto made it unthinkable, but the compounding crises of the Second World War, deep drought and a 'panicking' city agitated otherwise.[15]

FOUNDATION OBLIVION

A key condition of dams is that they make themselves felt far beyond the immediate context of their built form. Functions of a wider structure – the watershed – they are shaped by and in turn shape a causal horizon so large it is beyond human sensation. The dam built on the Warragamba River was no different. Where this dam departs is perhaps the extreme violence that accompanied its construction, which began soon after survey work was completed in 1946.[16]

First, in order to minimize potential flood debris in the form of dead tree trunks, the whole of the land upriver of the dam expected to be underwater was clear-felled (**FIG. C**). This extraordinary act of ecocide is today unremembered; indeed, the evidence of this act was obscured by the very thing by which it was justified: the impounded waters of the dam. But photographs from the valley floor, taken to document gravestones yet to be removed, incidentally reveal the destruction: a necrodatum, appearing like an intimation of the coming water (**FIG. D**).

As the valley rang with saws and tractors, the walls of the river's sandstone gorge were seeded with gelignite and vaporized. One worker tells of how, during this time, bird breeding in the area became impossible, as the vibrations from the detonations would fatally disrupt embryonic birds in their shells.[17] It is unlikely that these birds' wild cousins (and the egg-laying mammals) of Burragorang were spared. In this sense, these animals suffered a double slaughter: losing first their habitat, then their young.

While these preliminary works unfolded, other works to support the site were established beside it, including pumping stations, a refrigeration plant, ropeways to convey aggregate from a mine on the Nepean twenty-one kilometres away, access bridges and the new township, named Warragamba, which comprised hundreds of pre-fabricated houses, a school, a picture theatre, a fire service, a medical centre, a dance hall and a 'wet' canteen (the pub). Then, like a great, cooperative worm, labourers began to cut a bypass tunnel through the sandstone of the valley, an auxiliary waterway that was to be the Warragamba River's final, unmodulated course. Coffer dams were built at either end of the future building's footprint, clearing the site for the dam's foundations. As the labourers cut and blasted down, the sandstone moved; relieved of the weight of 2.3 million tonnes of younger strata, it welled upwards to meet them.[18] But once the bed was shaped and dry, the bells of the dogmen spoke and concrete began to pour.[19] The process was continuous. Buckets of aggregate arrived along the ropeway every thirty seconds for seven years.[20] Hoppers hauled on the cableway swung into place to cast 'blocks' – modules so large they needed ice mixed into their slurry lest a runaway exothermic reaction cause them to explode (**FIG. B**).

(New York: Palgrave Macmillan, 2010). See also William Cronon, "The Trouble with Wilderness; or, Getting Back to the Wrong Nature," originally in *Uncommon Ground: Rethinking the Human Place in Nature,* ed. idem (New York: W. W. Norton & Co., 1995), 69–90.

12 Note for readers outside of Australia: within Australia, Country (always capitalized) is the Indigenous Australian conception of Earth's interconnected lands, skies and waters and the living and non-living entities that inhabit them. It is a deeply specific concept inalienable to Aboriginal Australian ontologies; but through spoken and written Acknowledgements of Country, ceremonial Welcomes to Country, and urban planning policies such as Connecting with Country, non-Indigenous uses of the word, if not the limits of any appreciations of it, have become commonplace.

13 Mar, "National Parks and the Unsettling of Emptied Lands" (see note 11), 85; see also the work of Bruce Pascoe, Bill Gammage and Marcia Langton.

B

LEFT
Warragamba Dam under construction, showing the concrete modules or 'blocks,' *c.* 1950–60. Image: Sydney Water/WaterNSW archives.

Eventually, three million tonnes of concrete were poured, pushing back the sandstone like a merciless thumb.[21] From this work came constant noise; the clang of metal and stone, the gurgle of pneumatic vibrators; the crunch of boots on scree.

As before, the concrete works of the dam were attended by legislative updates to secure its catchment. This came via a proclamation in the Government Gazette on September 4, 1942; and, as before, the shape of the catchment was given in a continuous, geodetic ramble that, should one have wanted, could have been spoken aloud:

> Commencing at the junction of Megarrity's Creek with the Warragamba River and extending thence north-westerly to the common boundary of the Wollondilly and Blue Mountains Shires; thence generally westerly and north-westerly by that boundary and a northerly continuation to a reserved road 150 links wide in portion 23, parish of Kedumba, county of Cook; thence by that road and road catalogued R. 1,502-1,603, road 75 links wide, road catalogued 1,452-1,603, and a reserved road 50 links wide generally northerly to the Main Western Highway; thence westerly by that highway to a road in portion 29, parish of Megalong, county of Cook; thence by that road south-westerly to Megalong Creek in portion 148 of the said parish of Megalong; thence generally westerly by that creek to its junction with Cox's River; thence southerly by that river ...[22]

Despite coming decades after the Upper Nepean Scheme, no more meaningful regard was given to the Indigenous custodians of the valley, the Gundungurra, whose homes and sacred spaces were doomed to be flooded, although work in constructing the dam, and thus having a hand in the destruction of their own cultural practices, was offered.[23] Scarcely more regard was given to either the descendants of white settlers or the war-time immigrants who had made the river valley their home, such as the Meyer family – German Jewish refugees who had arrived in Australia in the 1940s, had moved into the valley and who, in the decade and a half it took to plan and construct of the dam, had made the valley their home.[24] As the papers stated at the time, the Water Board was a "law unto itself"; when the time came for the valley to be evacuated, there was no consultation or public inquiry.[25]

To this day, the former residents of the flooded township meet once a year, to restore for an evening the form of that community, united by an abiding sense of loss; a loss that, as in countless other spaces of the settler-colonial project, is itself turning upon the foundational and unimaginable loss of Burragorang's Traditional Owners.

Oskar Frederick Johanson

EFFECTS AND EXCESS

When the dam was complete, a body of water began to form behind it, and the wreckage that had been made of the valley was obscured. The water behind the dam was named 'Lake Burragorang,' but in many ways this is a misnomer; owing to its highly confected nature, little overturning occurs throughout the water column, and its benthic zone is reportedly lifeless.[26] Unhaunted by even the bravest of eels, more tomb than lentic body, this space is soundless except for the hydro-phonic signal of the dam itself: its grumbles as it flexes with changes in temperature and pressure; the hiss of the water where it is drawn off through a screen.

These conditions are not sensible from the visitor centre. Instead, it is the dam's techno-sublimity and its majestic context that has made it a modest tourist attraction and a handy badge for its operators looking to justify their existence (**FIG. F**). In the narrative

14 Sketch plans for a dam were reportedly developed as early as 1845. "Dams of Greater Sydney and Surrounds: Warragamba," *Water*NSW (2015): 6.

15 Donald Hector, "Sydney's Water Sewerage and Drainage System," *Journal & Proceedings of the Royal Society of New South Wales* 144 (2011): 3–25.

16 Note that works such as the Warragamba Emergency Scheme had actually already begun on the Warragamba River at an earlier date – but this much smaller dam was designed to be superseded by the coming Warragamba Dam proper.

17 *Warragamba: A Story of Our Making,* produced for WaterNSW by Free Range Media, 2016, 21:31 min. Available at the visitor centre and also online: youtube.com/watch?v=UzkiKW_Yl1U (accessed August 6, 2024).

18 WaterNSW, Warragamba Dam visitor centre permanent exhibition, February 2024.

19 'Dogmen' directed cranes from the ground to either hoist, stop or lower their loads.

20 WaterNSW, February 2024 (see note 18).

21 Ibid.

22 "Metropolitan Water, Sewerage and Drainage Act, 1924–1941," *Government Gazette of the State of New South Wales* (Sydney, NSW: 1901–2001), September 4, 1942, p. 2499, nla.gov.au/nla.news-article225109707 (accessed March 4, 2024).

23 As told by Gundungurra Elder Kazan Brown, in an interview with Dr Siwan Lovett, "How Will Raising the Warragamba River Wall Erase Indigenous Heritage?" on the podcast *Take Me to the River,* Australian River Restoration Centre, 2021, arrc.au/podcast-take-me-to-the-river/episode-13-how-will-raisingthe-warragamba-dam-wallerase-indigenous-heritage/).

24 Oskar Johanson, interview with Max Meyer, February 2024.

25 "Warragamba Dam," *The Farmer and Settler* (Sydney, NSW: 1906–1955), May 8, 1941: 1, nla.gov.au/nla.news-article117171625 (accessed March 1, 2024).

26 Interview with WaterNSW staff.

C

D

C Burragorang Valley clear-felled, *c.* 1945–55. The area that has been cleared represents the predicted water level of the reservoir. Image: Sydney Water/WaterNSW archives.

D Graves marked to be re-interred, Burragorang Valley, *c.* 1945–55. The edge of the trees above represents the future water level. Image: Sydney Water/WaterNSW archives.

Oskar Frederick
Johanson

that greets visitors to the site, much is made of the fact that the dam, through the security apparatus of the Special Areas (as the protected catchment areas are now known), actively protects its surrounding environment, to say nothing of the sacred Gundungurra sites of the valley that were not flooded by the original scheme (but which may yet be flooded should the dam wall be raised).[27] In other words, the immense and traumatic intrusion of the dam into the valley was the best thing that could have happened to it.

But the rock remembers. And the water moving through and around the dam indexes its every effect for those who choose to hear it.

Despite the scale and audacity of the dam, new works continued throughout the twentieth century, including those that form part of the Shoalhaven Scheme. This scheme intercepts and detains the waters of the Shoalhaven watershed, the southern extent of which is 275 kilometres south of Sydney; yet through pipes and pumps, its waters are mechanically connected to the Nepean and ultimately the faucets of Sydney. In this way, the combined works massively expand what could be called the city's hydro-causal horizon, a trans-territorial form by which the effects of the city are made to be felt. Insofar as the water in these pipes and reservoirs is a contiguous medium, resonant with mechanical transmissions, we can think of this scheme as a kind of extracochlear urbanization of the bush.

Warragamba Dam itself was not immune to modification: in the late 1980s, the dam wall was raised by five metres, creating a new white stratum along its top edge that can clearly be seen today. This raising was done ostensibly to 'strengthen' the wall, but also to try to address the great paradox of the dam: that while its first function was to supply water to the city – and thus it must always aim to be full – its second function has become that of flood water mitigation – a function it cannot achieve if full. This second function has legitimated development in the floodplains below it, which in an additional, deeper paradox has only increased the city's dependency on ever more desperate flood mitigation **(FIG. E)**.[28] These nested paradoxes remain unresolved and are why, whenever big storms descend on Sydney, media attention focuses on the dam and the inevitable turning of its gates, when gigalitres of water are let out into the river below, and the dam begins to scream.

Few of us will have a chance to stand above the dam gates during one of these release events, when the water above the gate floor is being measured in metres. But we can each imagine the building in that moment, humming like a three-million-tonne timpani. To do so is to consider the transmissions of another world, a riverworld, at once circumvolant (*circum* and laminal); held apart, but hopelessly all-surrounding and all-entangling. It is to experience what Clemens Finkelstein would call a "resonance" with this riverworld – a moment of vibrational sympathy by which a much larger but usually imperceptible structure can be sensed[29] – and, by extension, every story of the rock through which that world has passed: the spent hammers and the dogmen's bells; the fallen trees and the ruined eggs; the Meyers's piano, still in the old house, silent in the silent water. •

27 Less still is made of the fact that should Traditional Owners want to walk their own land they must be chaperoned by a WaterNSW officer.

28 As of April 2024, the State Government of NSW has indicated its willingness to invest in desalination capacity in order to draw down the permanent storage level of the dam. This comes off the back of an election commitment to not increase the dam wall height, as was the preference of the former administration and the real-estate industry.

29 Clemens Finkelstein, "Vibrascapes, Contact Zones and Planetary Media," *KoozArch*, July 10, 2022, koozarch.com/essays/vibrascapes (accessed August 6, 2024).

E The southern wall of the dam spillway. After a major storm event, part of the sandstone wall collapsed and was refaced and reinforced by these terraces of concrete. Photo: Oskar Johanson.

F A memorial cube of large-aggregate concrete, representative of the material out of which Warragamba Dam is constructed. Photo: Oskar Johanson.

Contributors

YUMNA AL-ARASHI is a Yemeni-Egyptian-American artist working with both still and moving images. Her practice critically reflects on the ways in which images shape the world we live in. Her first monograph, *Aisha*, will be published by Edition Patrick Frey in the autumn of 2024. She is currently based in Zürich.

MATHILDE REDOUTÉ is a French architect engaged in designing, writing and teaching. Her research explores the impact of governance on spatial dynamics, informed by concepts such as commoning, enclosures and wasteland. Having previously worked for Junya Ishigami in Tokyo, she is currently completing her PhD at the Architectural Association School of Architecture (AA) in London.

AKSHAR GAJJAR is an architect and urban designer, currently based at the Swiss Federal Institute of Technology Lausanne. His research transects architecture, urbanism, ecology and queer studies. His current monograph project "Better together: More-than-human ecologies for architectural thinking," examines post-industrial ruins for their potential in multispecies' collaborative survival.

BHAVYA JAIN is a student at Harvard University Graduate School of Design, where her research focuses on ecological adaptation and urban resilience strategies. She is the co-founder of blurck21, a design practice in India.

VALENTINA NOCE is the founder of Sabotage Practice, an architectural studio based in Milan. Established in 2023, the studio works on private projects and consultancies. While completing a PhD in Architecture at the Politecnico di Milano, Noce conducts research, lectures and teaches.

STEFAN BREIT is a trained environmental scientist and works as a lecturer and researcher at the Chair of Being Alive at ETH Zürich. His work focuses on the regeneration of landscapes and the design of nature-based approaches for a net-zero society.

INSA JELENA STREIT studied architecture in Berlin and Copenhagen and holds a MSc in Architecture from ETH Zürich. While studying for her master's degree, she worked as a research assistant at the Chair of Being Alive.

NEGAR SANAAN BENSI is an assistant professor at the Architecture faculty at TU Delft and the chair of Borders & Territories. Her publications include *Datapolis: Exploring the Footprint of Data on Our Planet and Beyond, Footprint #23:*

The Architecture of Logistics (co-editor), and the upcoming book *An Inhabitable Infrastructure: Rethinking the Architecture of the Bazaar.*

ELNAZ NAJJAR NAJAFI holds a PhD in architecture from Shahid Beheshti University (SBU), Faculty of Architecture and Urban Development. She is a member of the Advisory Board at The Research Institute of Iran Cultural Heritage and the [co]author of several books, including *Namak-nameh: Essays on Iranian Gusto* and *Where is Iran? Who is an Iranian? A Cultural Theory.*

STAVROULA MICHAEL has recently completed her PhD in History and Theory of Architecture, focusing on water infrastructures and conflict in colonial and post-colonial Cyprus at the University of Cyprus, where she has also taught architectural history and theory. Since 2024, Michael has taught at Minjiang University in Fuzhou, China, and was nominated as a member of the Society of Architectural Historians' Affiliate Group "Women in Architecture."

LUCIA REBOLINO, a researcher at Forensic Architecture in London and Columbia University in New York, explores new counter-cartography practices. She holds an MArch from Politecnico di Torino and an MSc in Computational Design from Columbia University.

FEDERICA PESSOTTO shapes visual narratives in art, fashion and photography as an art director at Studio Lys in Milan. She holds an MArch from Politecnico di Torino and an MFA in Set Design from the Rome University of Fine Arts.

LINDA SCHILLING CUELLAR is a PhD candidate at the Center for Research Architecture at Goldsmiths, University of London. Her research focuses on the commodification of nature through the lens of environmental policy protocols like Environmental Impact Assessments. She holds an MSc in Urban Design from Columbia University and an undergraduate degree in Architecture from Universidad Técnica Federico Santa María, in Chile.

OSKAR FREDERICK JOHANSON is a designer, writer and PhD candidate at Norwegian University of Science and Technology. Since 2021, he has been co-program head of the AA Visiting School Sydney. From 2021–22 he was an Agent of Change for the 10th Architecture Biennale Rotterdam. He graduated from AA diploma unit 19, has taught at the University of Sydney and the AA, and has written for *AA Files* and *The Avery Review*, among others.

DELUS
Journal for Landscape and Urban Studies

DELUS is an interdisciplinary publication on landscape and urban studies by the Institute of Landscape and Urban Studies, ETH Zürich.

Issue 1
Autumn 2024

FOUNDING EDITORS
Sara Frikech, Johanna Just

PROJECT MANAGEMENT
Dorothee Hahn

COPYEDITING
Irene Schaudies
Liana Simmons

GRAPHIC DESIGN
Studio Folder

PRODUCTION
Alise Ausmane, Hatje Cantz

REPRODUCTIONS
LONGO AG · SpA, Italy

PRINTING AND BINDING
Livonia Print, Riga

PAPER
Magno Volume, 150 g/m²

TYPOGRAPHY
Styrene B (Berton Hasebe and Ilya Ruderman, 2016)
Louize (Matthieu Cortat, 2011)

PUBLISHED BY
Hatje Cantz Verlag GmbH
Mommsenstraße 27
10629 Berlin
Germany
www.hatjecantz.com
A Ganske Publishing Group Company

ISBN 978-3-7757-5874-1
ISBN ePDF 978-3-7757-5875-8
ISSN 2941-6515
ISSN ePDF 2941-6531

Printed in Latvia

COVER ILLUSTRATION
Yumna Al-Arashi, 2023

Significant support is provided by the Institute of Landscape and Urban Studies, ETH Zürich.

THANKS TO
Tom Avermaete
Teresa Galí-Izard
Michiel van Iersel
Freek Persyn
Sabine Sarwa

DELUS

lus.arch.ethz.ch
@delusjournal
delus@arch.ethz.ch